SAN FRANCISCO:GRAPHIC DESIGN

SAN FRANCISCO:GRAPHIC DESIGN

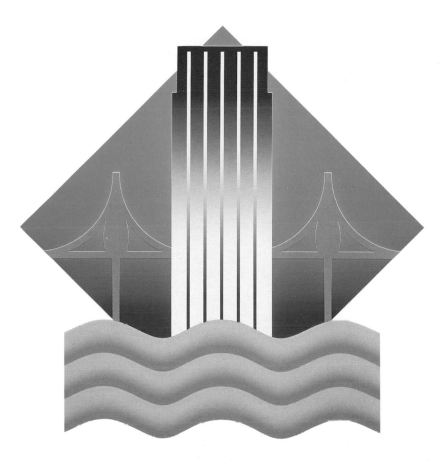

Designed and Edited by
GERRY ROSENTSWIEG

Written by
BARBARA FERNANDEZ

Introduction by
MICHAEL VANDERBYL

Editorial photography by
R.J.MUNA

Published by
MÁDISON SQUARE PRESS

ISBN 0-942604-29-6
Library of Congress Catalog Card Number 92-061451

Distributors to the trade in the United States and Canada:
Van Nostrand Reinhold 115 Fifth Avenue, NY 10003

Distributed throughout the rest of the world by:
Hearst Books International 1350 Avenue of the
Americas
New York, NY 10019

Publisher:
Madison Square Press 10 East 23rd Street, New York,
NY 10010

Editor: Gerry Rosentswieg
Designer: The Graphics Studio

PRINTED IN HONG KONG

CONTENTS

6

PREFACE

San Francisco is one of the most beautiful cities in the world. It is a rich, port city, cross cultured and tolerant, a city built on a human scale, accessible and intimate. It is a city that respects its history and tradition while it builds its future. The old time businesses that flourished are still there, supplemented by new high-tech industries, and the international market. The city has a well defined cultural life and a well-known fine arts community.

Urban San Francisco is geographically smaller than most major cities in this country. This compactness fosters an unusually strong sense of community. Most of the studios featured in this book are within a twenty block range of each other and the principals meet and phone each other regularly. There are restaurants where it is not unusual to see two or three tables of designers at lunchtime. There are saloons where the conversations are as likely to be about Bodoni and Garamond as the Giants or Forty-Niners. The rivalries are friendly.

As you look through this book, you'll see a volume of exciting new work, a broad range of work for national and international clients, as well as a larger than normal proportion of pro bono projects that benefit the arts and social fabric of the community. You'll also note that many of the larger clients, based in the city and surrounding suburbs, divide their work between the many fine studios.

It is not surprising that most of the designers are transplants who have chosen to live in this beautiful city. What is surprising is the depth and breadth of work that comes out of this "small town"-- San Francisco: Graphic Design presents thirty-two top design firms exploring every facet of graphic design. Enjoy!

Gerry Rosentswieg

INTRODUCTION

San Francisco is a unique city, balancing precariously
at the western edge of the continent. Although the spirit
of this place is more than a matter of terrain, geography
at least in part defines its features. As a community of
graphic designers, we participate in the city's character
and its' contradictions -- culturally diverse and yet
provincial, honoring tradition and yet wide open in it's
embrace of the new, the untried, and the eccentric.

Do we, as graphic artists, share an identity other than
residence in a western outpost of the United States?
In making general statements about design, it is too easy
to distort a complex body of work into evidence of more or
less arbitrary geographic or historical themes that
satisfy our need for order. Rather than a stylistic unity,
it is our community of graphic designers that distinguishes
our town from New York, Los Angeles and other cities.

There is in San Francisco a friendly dialogue, that includes
dissension as well as consensus, not found elsewhere.
Designers have tended to roost together in low rent neighborhoods,
creating a proximity that encourages the perception of
a common life, if not a common aesthetic.

Our community is also unique in its relative local weight.
Designer density is high. The city supports studios with
commissions for signage, exhibit design and product
design, as well as labels for California wines, menus for
cafes, and interiors for local shops. Design has been more
easily recognized as a cultural force thanks to the
unusual range and penetration of design activity into
the urban landscape.

All cities enjoy cultural diversity, but San Francisco designers
draw from unusually eclectic sources. There is no <u>School</u>
with its implication of master, apprentices and doctrines.
Rather, our profession thrives as a collective of individuals
with common concerns and inevitable frictions. By embracing
diversity, we have created a community. The work in this book
is evidence of the richness and vitality of that community.

Michael Vanderbyl

AKAGI / REMINGTON DESIGN

14

Akagi/Remington Design sits in the heart of San Francisco's financial district serving the design needs of everyone from architects and engineers to wineries, the arts, high-tech companies and banks.

Silicon Valley companies like Apple Computer, Adobe Systems, Sun Microsystems and National Semiconductor have sought their expertise in point of sale and packaging design, while San Francisco's Museum Society, Chamber Symphony, and Film and Video Arts Commission look to Akagi/Remington Design for quarterly publications, identity and ad campaigns.

Doug Akagi has spent 29 years designing marketing communications, packaging, corporate identity and environmental graphics. For 15 years partner Dorothy Remington has specialized in illustration and editorial design as well as corporate identity and communications.

"We like to think our work stands the test of time," says Doug Akagi. "Hopefully it has depth and content as well as esthethic - so it doesn't go in one eye and out the other," he jokes.

1

1. Akagi/Remington staff.
2 - 3. Corporate brochure for
U.S. Windpower, Inc.

2

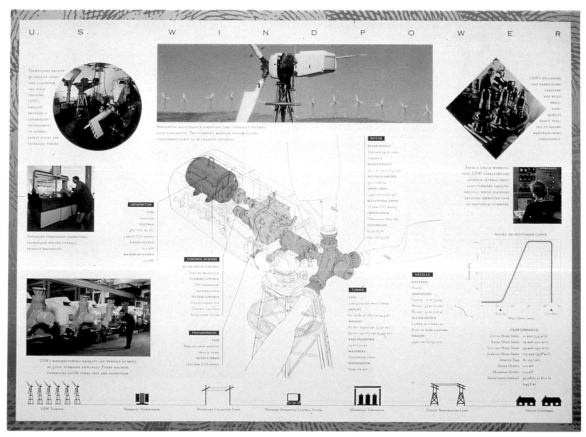

3

18

1

1. Wine label for California Wine Marketing, Inc.
2. Quarterly publication for the San Francisco Museum Society.

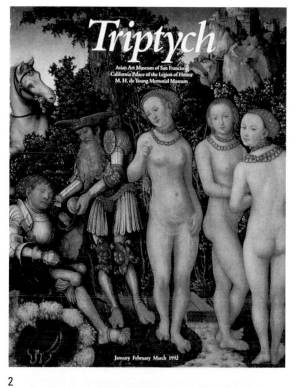

Triptych

Asian Art Museum of San Francisco
California Palace of the Legion of Honor
M. H. de Young Memorial Museum

January·February·March 1992

2

JANUARY · FEBRUARY · MARCH 1992

Triptych

THE MUSEUMS

Asian Art Museum of San Francisco
The Avery Brundage Collection
Rand Castile, Director

The Fine Arts Museums of San Francisco
California Palace of the Legion of Honor
M. H. de Young Memorial Museum
Harry S. Parker III, Director

MUSEUM HOURS:
Wednesday through Sunday, 10 AM –
5 PM. The Asian Art Museum and the
M.H. de Young Memorial Museum are open
until 8:45 PM on Wednesday, January 8,
Wednesday, February 5, and Wednesday,
March 4.

All three museums are closed on New Year's
Day, Martin Luther King, Jr. Day, and Presidents Day.

ADMISSION:
Members of The Museum Society   Free
Adults 18-64 $5
Seniors (65 & older) $3
Ages 12-17 $2
Under 12   Free

The First Wednesday and first Saturday
morning of each month are free.

MEMBERS' MORNINGS:
8:30-10 AM. Free. Membership card required.
January 18, California Palace of the Legion of
Honor; March 21, M.H. de Young Memorial
Museum.

TELEPHONE NUMBERS:
Asian Art Museum
    668-8921 (switchboard)
    668-6404 (programs)
The Fine Arts Museums
    750-3600 (switchboard)
    863-3330 (Hotline)
    750-7667 (box office)
The Museum Society Membership Office
    750-3636
The Museum Stores
    750-3642 (de Young and Legion)
    296-4035 (at Macy's)

FRONT AND BACK COVERS: The Judgement of Paris by Lucas Cranach the Elder (German, 1472–1553). Oil distemper on limewood, 24 1/2" x 15 1/4" Joannneum Graz, Alte Galerie, BG 17". From the exhibition, Imperial Austria: Art, Arms, and Armor from the State of Styria. The armor worn by Paris is typical of the early 16th century, but Mercury's fantastic costume is Cranach's imaginative attempt to suggest the antique. To read more about art and armor, see page 14.

FACING PAGE: Photograph by Paul Franz Moore (floral style). Michaela Thiesen. The 8th annual Bouquets to Art and the held March 10 to 14, 1992. See page 2 for information about this benefit event, which coincides with the exhibition Art, Arms, and Armor. Use the order form facing page 44.

Triptych No. 60
Pamela Forbes, Editor
Barbara Traisman, Feature Writer
Sangi/Remington, Design
Printed by Cal Central Press

Triptych is published by The Museum Society,
M. H. de Young Memorial Museum, Golden
Gate Park, San Francisco, California 94118.

20

1

1. Point of purchase poster
for Opcode Systems.
2-3. Packaging for Opcode
Systems, music software
and hardware.

2

3

PRIMO ANGELI

22

1

2

3

4

A veritable supermarket of packaging designs sits on shelves at Primo Angeli Inc. Orville Redenbacher popcorn, Quaker Instant Oats, Kraft BBQ Sauce, Henry Weinhard, Coors and Miller beers, and San Francisco's own Boudin Sour Dough French bread, all dressed in Angeli designs.

Packaging such well known brand names makes for design decisions that "can mean multi-million dollar changes in sales results — up or down," says Angeli. "We're paid to communicate and get a positive response. You've got to touch somebody's heart with this stuff," he says.

The studio's consumer-friendly atmosphere includes an assortment of antique juke boxes in mint condition. His office displays a cardboard cutout of Primo in Oakland A's uniform, the uniform and sleeve patch bearing designs created to commemorate the 1987 All Star Game. "We only took credit for the design after they won the pennant," jokes Angeli.

Primo Angeli calls his 30-plus person design firm a conglomeration of highly creative people from all over the world. Their unique differences, he says, make for a habit of embracing what's different as an avenue to discovering what's successfully unique. "Our working philosophy is to be the best translators of marketing objectives into the most viable brand and packaging products.

5

1. Studio reception area.
2. Design studio.
3. Studio logo.
4. Primo Angeli.
5. 50th anniversary of U.S. savings
bonds postage stamp.
6. Golden Gate Bridge anniversary poster.
7. Columbus Day promotional poster.
8. Poster for San Francisco week
in Sydney, Australia.

6

7

8

24

1

2

3

4

5   6   7

8

9

1. Packaging for Henry Weinhard
Brewing Company.
2. Packaging for a non-alcoholic beer.
3. Promotional package.
4. Packaging for Pete's Brewing Company.
5 - 7. Packaging for Cambridge diet plan.
8. Iced tea packaging.
9. Promotional poster.

26

1

2

3

4

5

6

7

9

1. Packaging for an imported coffee line.
2. Packaging for a candy manufacturer.
3. Ice cream packaging.
4. Logo for Ampex.
5 - 6. Packaging for Just Desserts Bakery.
7. Packaging for a line of dried fruit.
8. Specialty store product development.
9. Signage and environmental graphics program for a building/shopping complex.

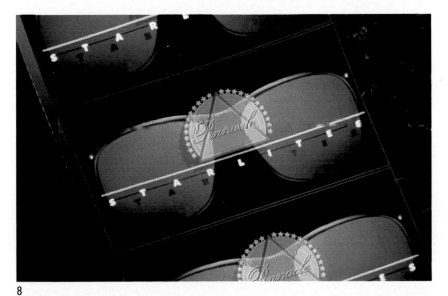

8

PRIMO ANGELI

590 Folsom Street, San Francisco 94105   415.974.6100   FAX 415.974.5476

28

3

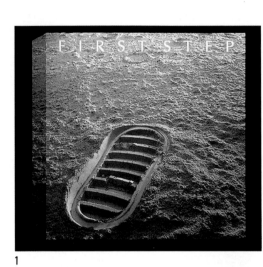

1

4

2

5

1 - 2. Software packaging.
3 - 4. Environmental graphics for
San Francisco Fashion Center.
5. Software packaging
design system.

BIELENBERG DESIGN

1

2

As you walk into Bielenberg Design a cafeteria sign displays the philosophical quote of the week. The words might read "We have met the enemy and he is us." - Pogo. Quotes, philosophy - IDEAS - drive Bielenberg Design.

Bielenberg Design has made a specialty of collateral brochures, annual reports, and corporate identity projects for the institutional investment business including clients; Shearson Lehman Advisors, Fidelity Management Trust Company, Transamerica Corporation, and MetLife.

Public service work for causes like Youth and Family Assistance and Under One Roof, the shop for AIDS relief, keeps Bielenberg Design involved in projects that have a mission.

John Bielenberg designed his open space studio, a place void of visual intrusions. "I want the project we're working on to be our sole focus," he says. White walls, suspended translucent glass panels and lots of sunlight offer the base on which Bielenberg Design creates work that communicates ideas.

3

4

5

THE PEOPLE WHO MAKE ART THEIR BUSINESS ARE MOSTLY IMPOSTERS.

-PABLO PICASSO

6

1-4. Studio interior.
5. Picasso quote used on stationery.
6. Capabilities brochure for Capital Consultants, a Portland investment firm .
7. Self-promotional moving announcement.
8. Line introduction brochure for Read Worth, a men's fashion designer.
9. Self-promotional brochure.

7

8

9

1

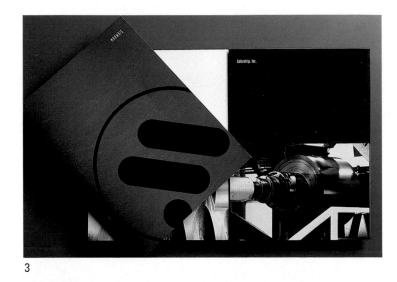

3

2

4

5

6

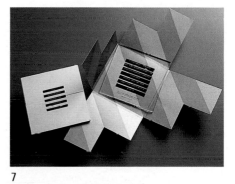

7

1. Stationery for Klein Design Group,
an advertising agency.

2. Identity package for Pareto Partners,
a quantitative investment firm.

3. Capabilities brochure for Marwais
Steel Company.

4. Financial software packaging
for Advent Software.

5. Hang tag for Woody & Worth,
environmentally conscious clothing.

6. Membership brochure for the
Corporate Design Foundation.

7. Wedding reception announcement.

8. The Shansby Group Annual Review.

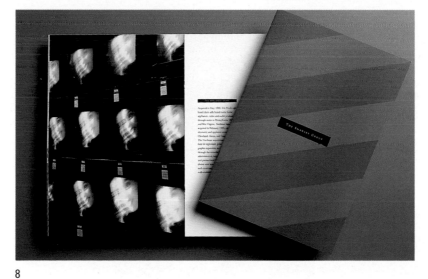

8

1

1. Capabilities brochure for Shearson
Lehman Advisors, an investment firm.
2.. Capabilities brochure for Investment
Advisors, a Houston Investment firm.
3. Hang tag for Alan Paine Sweaters.
4. Environmental poster for AIGA,
San Francisco Chapter.
5. Stationery for American Design
Intelligence Group, a fashion design studio.
6. 1990 Annual Report for Sunrise
Technologies, manufacturer of lasers
for medicine.
7. 1991 Annual Report for
Sunrise Technologies.

2

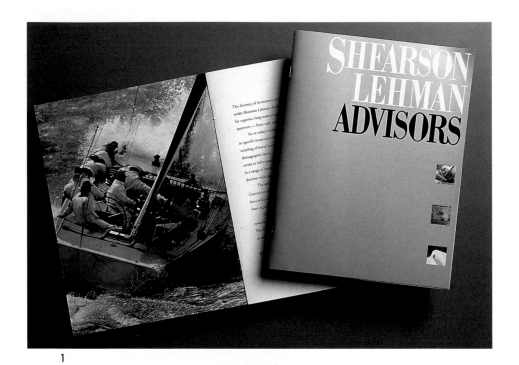

3

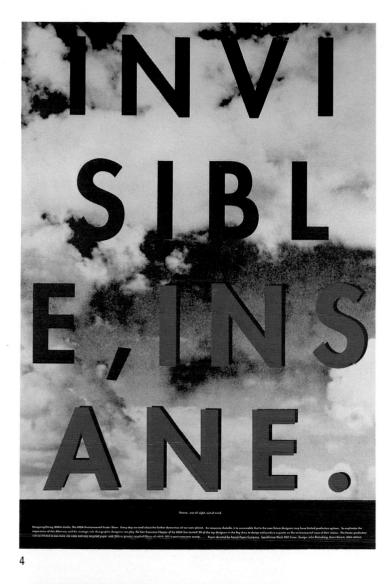

4

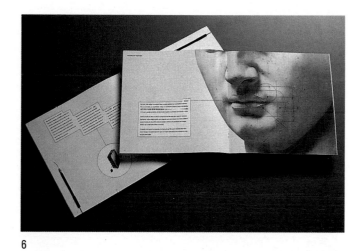

6

7

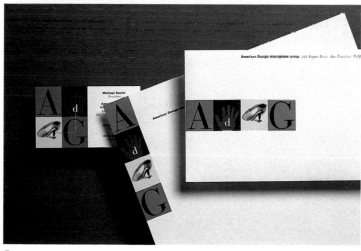

5

BIELENBERG DESIGN

333 Bryant Street, Suite 130, San Francisco 94107   415.495.3371   FAX 415.495.4842

36

1

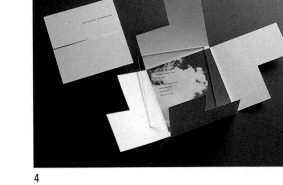

3

4

2

1. Capabilities brochure for Texas
Commerce Bank Investment Management.
2.. Capabilities brochure for Loomis Sayles,
an investment firm.
3. T-shirt design for Nike.
4. Housewarming party invitation.

TOM BONAURO DESIGN

Schooled in fine art, Tom Bonauro isn't daunted by traditional graphic design tenets. He doesn't mind using the work he does as a form of self expression.

"I see clients as commissioners of art," says Bonauro. "Only in this field four or five thousand people might see your work. It truly is public art," he continues.

"People come to me for my point of view," he says. Tom Bonauro's point of view or "esthetic" as he calls it, has satisfied the needs of everyone from Swatch International, to Levis, Esprit, Fox TV Network and Apple Computer.

"I view what defines an artist as how one thinks," comments Bonauro. "It's not what you do. It's how you see the world. People open windows to other people through their art."

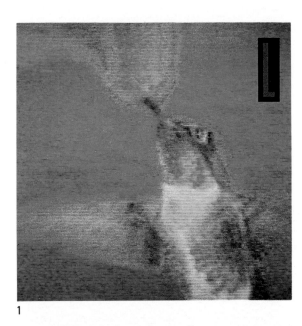

1

3

2

1. CD cover for "Lovenotes and Lithium."
2. CD cover for Voice Farm.
3. Album cover for Voice Farm.
4. Poster for the Diffa show house.
5. Invitation for Diffa show house benefit.
6 - 7. Business card for Fork in
the Road catering.
8. Record cover for "M."

4

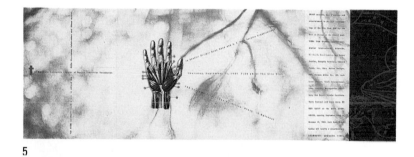

5

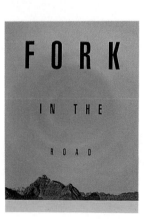

6

7

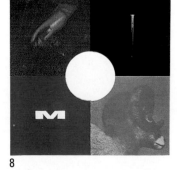

8

1

1. Business card for Herbaceuticals.
2. "Good Morning" poster for AIGA
exhibition on the environment.
3 - 4. Direct mail piece for MAC.
5. New year's card for MAC.
6. Direct mail piece for MAC; "Color Me MAC."

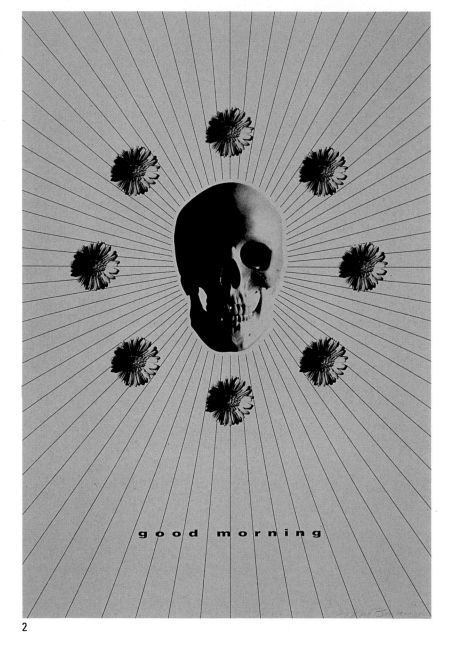

good morning

2

3

4

5

6

42

1 - 4. Pillow Talk greeting cards.
5. CD cover.
6 - 7. Invitation for a dog show
to benefit PAWS.
8 - 9. Greeting cards.
10. CD cover.

1

2

3

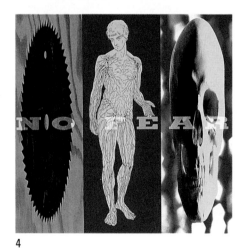

4

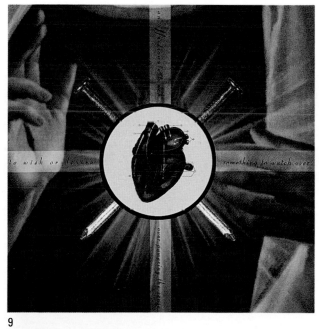

5

6

7

43

8

9

10

44

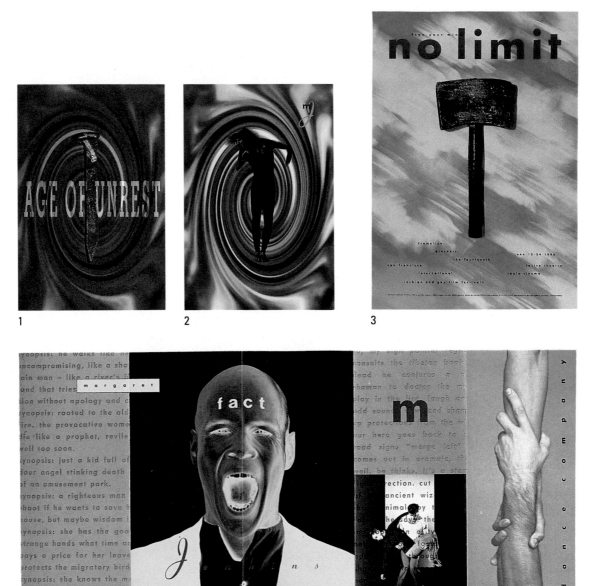

1

2

3

4

5

1 - 2. Covers of a brochure for the Margaret Jenkins Dance Company.
3. Poster for the Lesbian and Gay Film Festival.
4. Direct mail piece for a dance company.
5. Magazine insert.

ROSS CARRON DESIGN

46

1

In San Francisco's competitive design scene Ross Carron modestly admits he's not a very competitive person. Even so, for 15 years Carron Design has been attracting a wide range of clients, including wineries, toy companies, fashion manufacturers, publishers and architects.

"Diversity is what keeps it interesting to me," Carron says. "I love it when we get to work on food packaging, book design and corporate collateral all at the same time."

The client list at Carron Design includes Harper Collins Publishers, Navarro Vineyards, Sega of America, the California Academy of Sciences, Aviva Sports, Joe Boxer, and he laughs, "for four years I was the art director for the early Victoria's Secret catalog."

Schooled in architecture, Carron taught architectural design before teaching himself graphic design. With no portfolio or experience he landed a job as an art department trainee and six months later he was an art director.

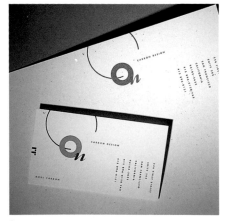

2

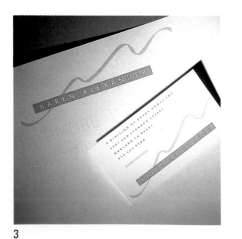

3

4

6

5

7

1. Ross Carron with design assistants Carole Jeung and Martin Heirakuji.
2. Carron Design identity.
3. Identity for Karen Alexander, a women's dress line.
4. Identity for S&Z/F+M, a joint venture architectural firm.
5. Promotional piece for Water, Inc., a women's sportswear line.
6. Ad series for S.P.UDZ, a boy's clothing line by Sweet Potatoes, Inc.
7. Caviar packaging for Polarica, Inc. a specialty foods importer.

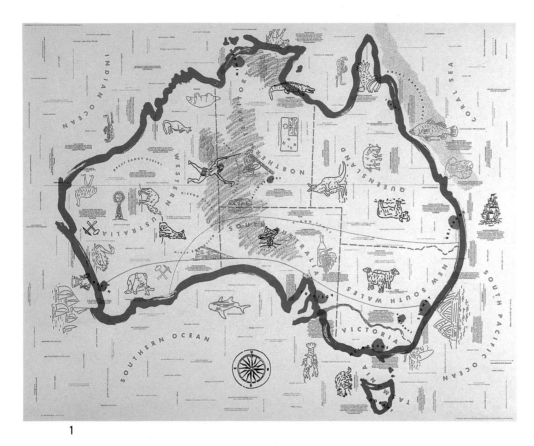

3

1. Disposable paper table covering for Wallaby's Australian restaurant.
2. Souvenir tour books sold at rock concerts.
3. Destination logo for DFS Group Ltd.
4. Catalog and promotional materials for Worlds of Wonder, a toy company.
5. Jump rope packaging.for Worlds of War
6. Poster for design symposium at California College of Arts and Crafts.

1

2

4

5

6

1

50

3

2

5

4

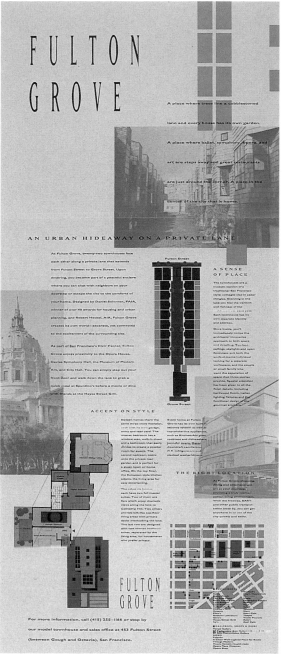

1. Identity for Tortola Restaurant featuring early California cuisine.

2. Packaging for Tortola Food Products.

3 - 4. Packaging for Navarro Vineyards.

5. Quarterly newsletters.

6. Sales brochure/poster for a condominium development.

7. Tasting room brochure for Gloria Ferrer Champagne Caves.

8 - 9. Research brochure for California Academy of Sciences.

6

8

9

52

1. Announcement card for Marin Apparel Company.
2. Packaging for Pepperwood Springs Winery.
3. Book cover for HarperSanFrancisco.
4. Promotional materials for Joe Boxer, apparel manufacturer.
5. Book cover for HarperSanFrancisco.
6. Poster for a two-person art exhibit.
7. Consumer ad for a women's dress line.
8. Poster for the Fine Arts Museum of San Francisco's exhibit of foot art.
9. Book cover for HarperSanFrancisco.

1

2

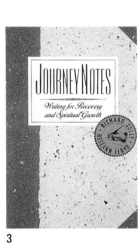

3

4

5

6

7

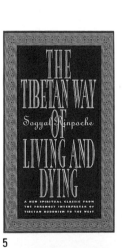

8

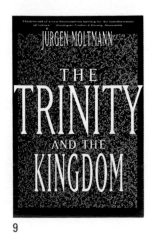

9

COLEMAN SOUTER

"People come to us because they see a great variety in our work, a diversity in our portfolio. That's because we try to let the client's problem direct our approach," says Mark Coleman.

In business since 1985, Coleman Souter's clients are as varied as their approach, ranging from the banking and financial industry to the performing arts, including four subscription campaigns for the San Francisco Opera that went from brochures to bus sides and billboards. "We try to keep a balance between corporate work and the creative arts," says Coleman.

On the corporate side, Coleman Souter's work includes design and consultation services for James River Corporation, Pacific Telesis and Bank of America. Rounding out the client roster are The San Francisco Zoo, Swatch International and a growing high tech list that includes both Apple Computer and Intel.

PHOTO: JOHN SUTTON

1

2

1. Interior of Coleman Souter.
2. Snack food packaging for American Grains.
3. Promotional sales kit for Sitka, software program.
4. Annual report for the San Francisco Zoo.
5. Symbol for Western Medical.
6. Halloween card for Coleman Souter.

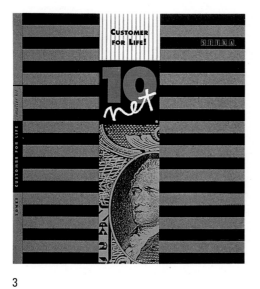

3

4

5

6

1

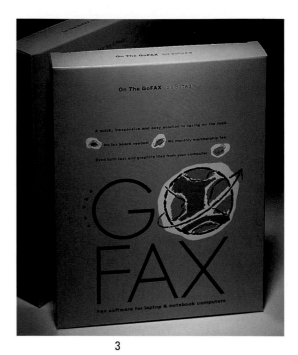

4

3

2

5   6

8

1-2. Spreads from Zoo Views, a periodical of the San Francisco Zoo.
3. Packaging for Ibis Corp., software program.
4. Valentine's Day card for Coleman Souter.
5. Trophy for James River's Best competition.
6 -7. Call for entries for James River Paper.
8. Subscription brochure for the San Francisco Opera.

58

1

2

3

4

5

7

1-2. Product catalog for
Burlington Denim's fall line.
3. Catalog for the annual San Francisco
Show design competition.
4. Identity for Roy hair salon.
5. Poster for the San Francisco
Ballet's production of Nutcracker.
6. Logotype for the San Francisco Opera.
7. Spread from a subscription brochure
for the San Francisco Opera.
8. Poster for the San Francisco
Opera's production of Lulu.

6

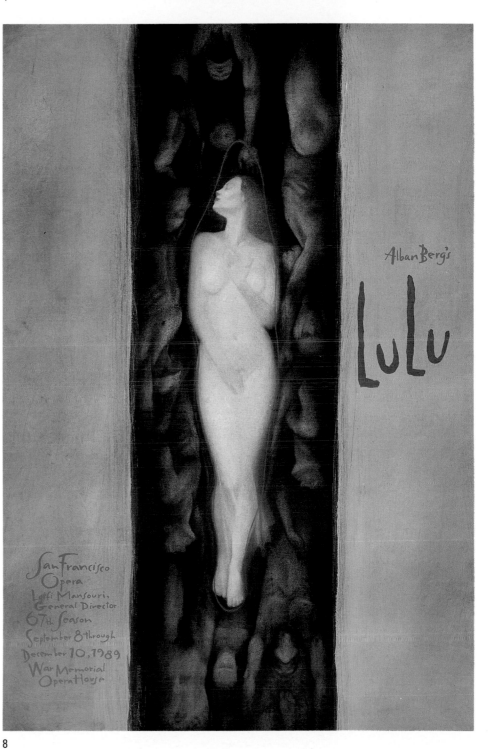

8

60

1

2

1. Automated teller machine card
for Bank of America.
2. Real estate loan brochure.
3. Annual report for
McKesson Corporation.
4. Logotype for Aegis, a real
estate syndicator.

4

McKESSON TODAY

JUNE 1991

"A Vision for the Future: Founded early in the 19th
century, McKesson approaches the 21st century firm in the
belief that our future prospects are enhanced by a sharper
focus on our core businesses. To realize this vision, the
employees of McKesson rededicate ourselves to doing better
what we do best:

"Distributing and marketing pharmaceuticals and health
and beauty care products and providing related retail,
hospital and managed prescription care services.

"Bottling, marketing and distributing pure drinking water."

3

MADELEINE CORSON DESIGN

Integrated is the word Madeleine Corson uses to describe her approach to design. An approach not only suitable to solving design problems, but also the happy result of working with San Francisco architect Richard Stacy to design a building that houses her studio, that of husband, photographer Thomas Heinser, and their home. Such close working quarters make integration of design and photography easy, as Corson and Heinser frequently collaborate for their varied clientele.

Whether a project is a high technology image or one of the many she's designed for the fashion industry, Corson finds the challenge of creating engaging communication equally intriguing. "The best designs are both visually and emotionally moving," she says.

Corson's book design for the U.S. National Park Service received not only the Federal Design Achievement Award but has become the format for many other Park Service publications.

Aside from designing books Corson is an avid reader, and often integrates her verbal side into design solutions. "It's when I'm reading," she says, "that ideas frequently come to me. The images practically paint themselves."

1

3

2

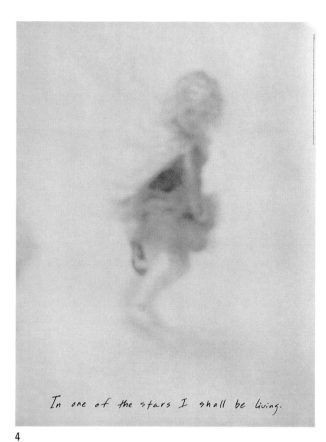

In one of the stars I shall be living.

4

1 - 2. 25 Zoe Street, a live/work space.
3. Studio logo.
4 - 6. Self-promotion poster series for
Madeleine Corson Design and Thomas
Heinser Photography Studio.

The thing that is important is
the thing that is not seen.

5

Looking up at the sky

Ask yourselves:

Is it yes or no

6

1

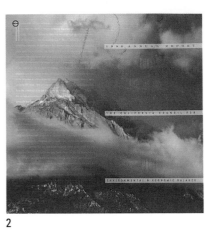

2

GROWTH MANAGEMENT

Public concern about California's ability to manage its phenomenal growth intensified in 1990 amidst reports that the growth has been faster than expected. This year the state's total population reached 30 million, and by the year 2000 it is likely to surpass 35 million. Meanwhile national media have begun asking whether the bloom was off the California flower. Hardly a day went by without media coverage of the growing homeless population, congested classrooms, our overburdened transportation network, environmental degradation, water shortages, or the flight of business out of the state. By the end of 1990, the jobless rate began to increase while real estate values declined, and the rift between the haves and the havenots widened. For the first time in recent memory, growth management received serious attention in the California gubernatorial campaign, as many citizens began to fear for our future social, environmental and economic quality of life in the Golden State.

3

AMNESTY INTERNATIONAL USA
HUMAN RIGHTS EDUCATION

5

1. Logo for Two Mean Gals, Inc.,
a western tour via wagon train
and horses.
2 - 3. Annual report for California Council for
Environmental and Economic Balance.
4. Logo for Amnesty International.
5. Fortune cookies, a self promotion piece
for Madeleine Corson Design and Thomas
Heinser Photography Studio.
6. Packaging and gift soaps for Eileen West.
7 - 8. Catalog for Eileen West, women's
apparel and home furnishings.

6

7

8

66

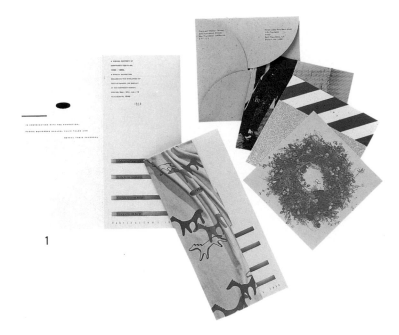

1

2

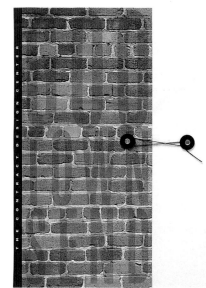

3

4

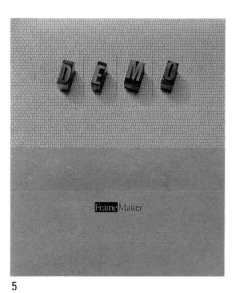

5

6

1. Direct mail event announcements for
Contract Design Center.
2 - 3. Presentation folder and brochure
for Contract Design Center.
4. Invitation to a symposium on
contract lighting.
5 - 6. Brochure for Frame Technology,
a publishing software program.
7. Software packaging for a word
processing software program.

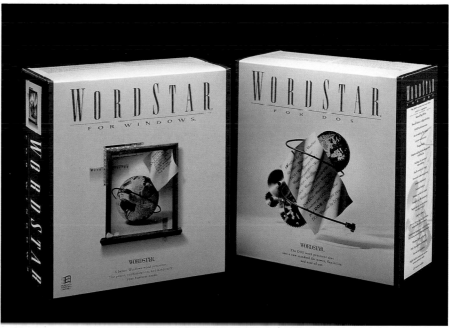

7

68

1. Calendar for Theater Artaud.
2. Catalog for Frame Technology.
3. Logo and letterhead system for Theater Artaud, a presenter of avant garde performance groups.

1

3

2

CRONAN DESIGN

70

Michael Cronan's studio is full of people who are good at organization but love chaos. People, he says, "who try to maintain a larger perspective."

That larger perspective pays off whether they're hard at work for Estee Lauder, LSI Logic or the Pickle Family Circus. The broad ranging client list at Cronan Design includes everything from retail and high-tech to Cronan's own Walking Man clothing line.

"San Francisco is a vital place for design," says Cronan. Finding it a city with unusual respect for design, he makes a regular practice of handling civic and arts related projects.

"For us design is a method of inquiry," says Cronan. "Design isn't a style, it's a way of seeing the world."

1

PHOTO: JOCK McDONALD

2

3

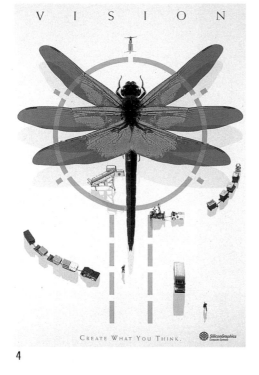

4

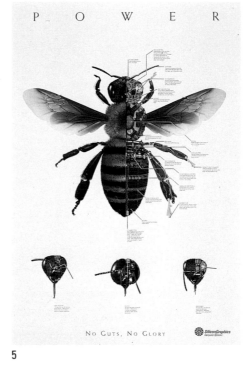

5

6

1. The Walking Man poster.
2. Michael Cronan as model in the Walking Man Clothing catalog. This line of clothing is designed and owned by Cronan Artefact.
3. Flag for Walking Man Clothing that flies over the studio.
4 - 6. Posters for Silicon Graphics.
7. Close-up of Color poster.

7

72

1

2

3

4

PHOTOS: JOCK McDONALD

5

1 - 4. Catalog images for Walking Man Clothing.
5. Icon depicting "challenge" for the Walking Man line.
6. Poster for the San Francisco symphony.
7 - 10. Catalog for Gary Fisher Bikes.

6

7

8

9

10

74

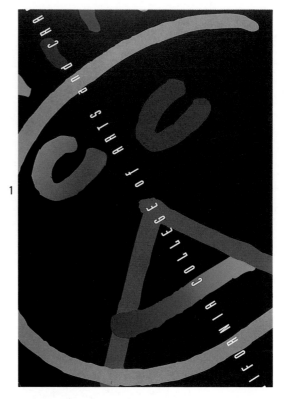

1

2

3

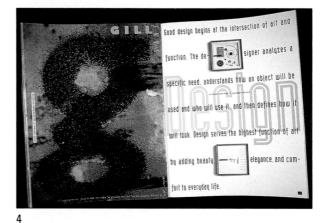

4

1 - 5. Cover and interior spreads for
California College of Arts and Crafts
view book and catalog.
6 - 11. Identity and package design
for an Estee Lauder line.

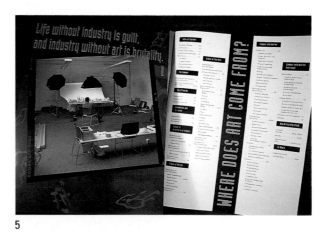

5

6

9

7

10   11

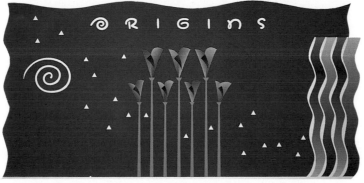

8

1

3

1. Poster for a typographer
depicting the "Forgotten Letters."
2. Original collage image for
Metropolitan Furniture.
3. Poster for the San Francisco
symphony.

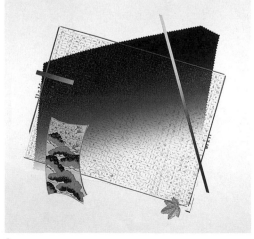

2

PAUL CURTIN DESIGN

Paul Curtin got his start in advertising when his job meant hiring San Francisco designers to flesh out his concepts. Today Curtin says he considers it a privilege to be held among the ranks of those designers.

Paul Curtin's "Say Hey" poster became a fixture behind Mayor Jordan as he made his last pitch to hold onto San Francisco's baseball team. Cocolat, of entrepreneurial and chocolate fame, counts on Paul Curtin Design for its tasty brand of packaging. And spirited ad campaigns for products like micro chips and cd rom have grabbed more than a little attention when Curtin attempts to "show intelligence through humor."

"My success lies in creating distinctive looks for my clients, not necessarily a distinctive look for my studio," says Curtin. "All clients have very different needs. Designers have to be versatile in how they relate with clients as well as the work they do," he continues.

3

1

2

4

6

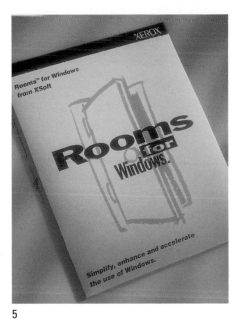

5

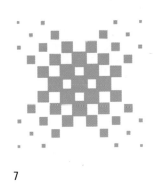

7

1. Display server packaging for
Lapis Technologies.
2. Promotional calendar for
artists' representative.
3. Studio logo.
4. CD software packaging.
5. Software packaging.
6. Video packaging for Visualiner.
7. Logo for Crosspoint Solutions.

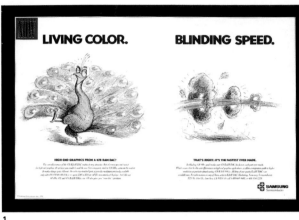

1

2

3

4

5

6

7

1 - 6. Advertising
campaign for Samsung.
7. Logo for Reardon &
Krebs Typographers.
8. Candy packaging.

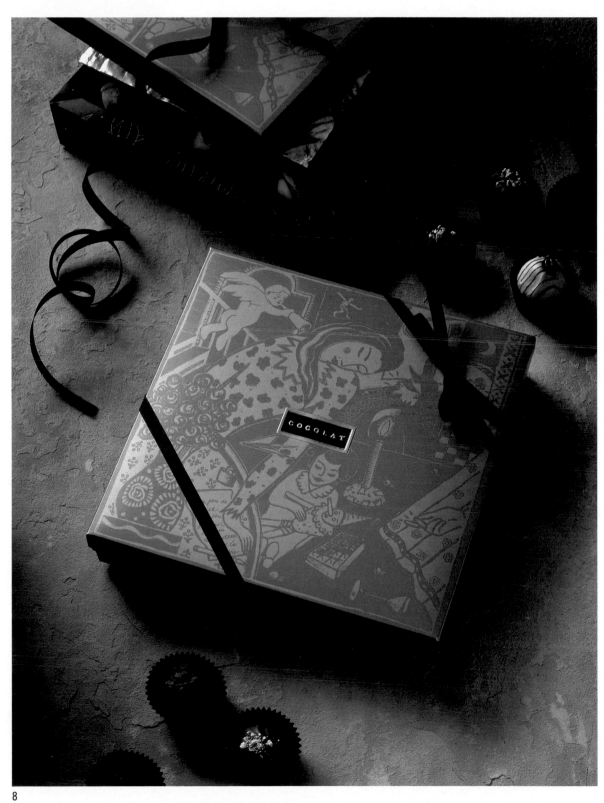

8

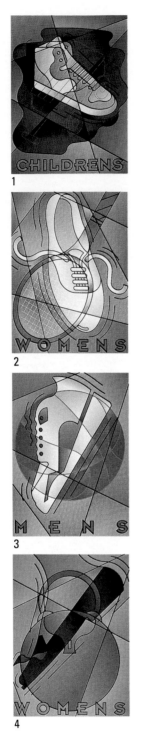

1

2

3

4

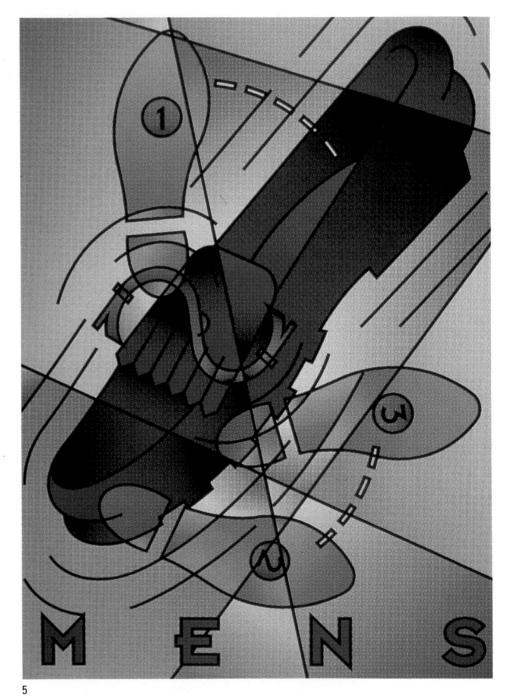

5

BICYCLE
TRAILS
COUNCIL

OF MARIN

8

6

9

1 - 5. Shoe department signage
for Mervyn's.
6. Wedding invitation.
7. Logo for Smart, modular technology.
8. Logo for Bicycle Trails Council.
9. Logo for Motto, furniture
manufacturers representatives.

SMART

7

84

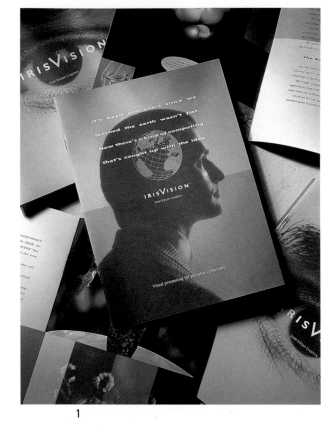

1

2

3

4

5

6

1. Identity and product capabilities brochure for Silicon Graphics.
2. German graphic card packaging for Hercules.
3. Logo and stationery.
4. Capabilities brochure and collateral.
5. Logo for Neil Ransick Marketing.
6. Logo for a mail order agriculture firm.

CURTIS DESIGN

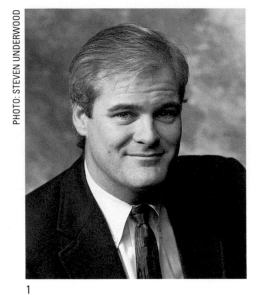

PHOTO: STEVEN UNDERWOOD

1

2

Three years ago when Dave Curtis formed Curtis Design he says "I started out as "CEO and janitor." A year later Dave Curtis matched his design and illustration talent with brother Brad's advertising expertise and Curtis Design became - Curtis Design.

The firm has since grown to a staff of five and Dave Curtis expects it to keep on growing. Seven years under the direction of Nicolas Sidjakov gave Dave Curtis what he calls "a good education in managing a fast growing firm while maintaining a high quality level of design." "Technology has changed the way we work, but the energy generated by bouncing ideas off each other remains a constant," he says.

Curtis Design started out with a focus on packaging design, helping to move products for San Francisco's Ghirardelli Chocolate Company, as well as companies such as Intel Corporation and Stroh Brewery. They've since expanded into identity, restaurant and environmental signage design. "Being small it can be a fight to get in the door," says Dave Curtis, "but once they see our work we usually come away with the job."

3

4

6

5

1. David Curtis.
2. Beer Logo.
3. Packaging for Miller Brewing Company.
4 - 6. Candy packaging.

1

MONTALBO'S
HOT BUTTERED RUM BATTER

2

4

BRENNAN'S
EST. 1959

3

5

Marin
Shake*fpeare
Company

6

VILLAGE

OVO

PEDDLER

8

1. Identity for a children's clothing retailer.
2. Logo for hot buttered rum mix.
3. Restaurant logo.
4. Packaging for Granny Goose.
5. Beer labeling system.
6. Identity for a theatrical company.
7. Poster design.
8. Identity for a bicycle retailer.

7

1

2

3

4

5

6

1. Restaurant identity.
2. Restaurant takeout packaging.
3 - 4. Software packaging.
5. Logo for a video game manufacturer.
6. Packaging for a home management
software program.
7. Identity for a vintage sports car retailer.
8. Logo for Cousin's Foods beef jerky.

8

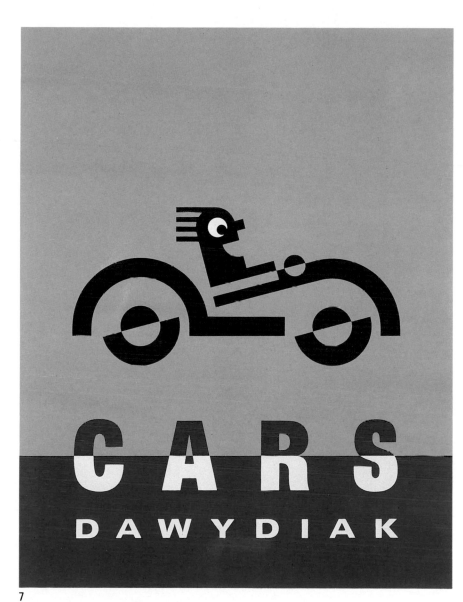

7

92

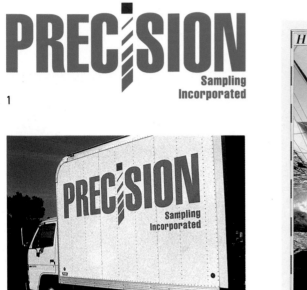

1

2

3

4

5

1 - 3. Identity for a soil sample
drilling company.
4 - 5. Sales literature for a sailing school
and yacht charter company.

MELANIE DOHERTY DESIGN

94

"If I could be a time traveler I'd travel back in time not forward," says Melanie Doherty. Her love of the past was kindled when she spent four years as a designer in Rome, Italy. There, centuries-old Baroque and rennaissance art was her muse as she worked for Bulgari, San Giorgio (Italy's largest olive oil producer) and international agencies Foote, Cone & Belding and McCann Erickson, among others.

Today Doherty enjoys the historical permanence of architecturally oriented projects like the environmental graphics for San Francisco's new Museum of Modern Art, or the signage system she's been asked to design, along with associate, architect Erin O'Reilly, for the City of Sacramento.

Packaging and print design are a big part of the Melanie Doherty Design picture. Williams-Sonoma, DFS, and the San Francisco Zoo are just a few of the clients served in that arena.

When Doherty's thoughts do travel to the future she hopes for more work that takes her to Rome, where one day she'd like to retire and learn the art of fresco restoration.

2

3

4

5

1

6

Porcelain

7

8

Linens & Flatware

9

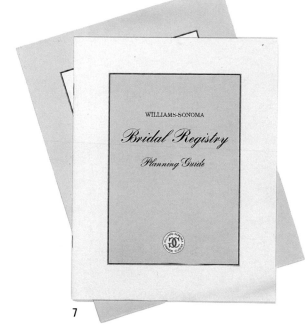

Bakeware

10

1. From left to right: Julie Willing, David Keram, Joan Folkmann, Melanie Doherty and Erin O'Reilly.
2. Logo for a chicken rotisserie restaurant.
3. Logo for an Italian leather handbag collection.
4. Crest for Lick-Wilmerding High School.
5. Logo for Squaw Creek Sports, a sporting goods boutique.
6. Restaurant logo.
7 - 10. Catalogue for Williams-Sonoma Bridal Registry.

1 - 2. Brochure for St. Supery Vineyards & Winery.
3. Mascot/Symbol for St. Supery.
4. Gift box and wine bottle.
5. Wine cases and wine bottles.
6. Newsletter and direct mail.
7. Winery collateral.

1

3

2

4

5

6

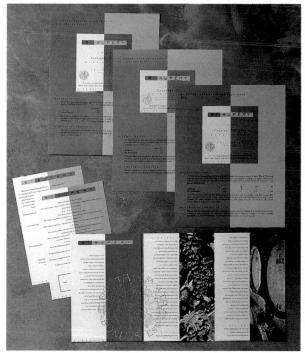

7

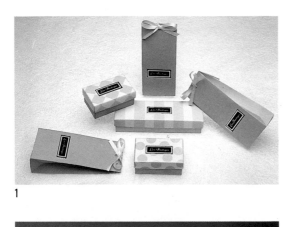

1

2

3

4

6

7

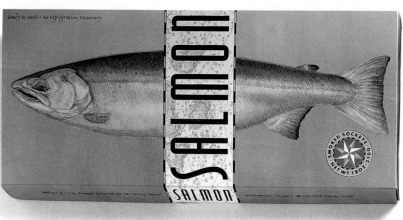

5

1. Packaging for Les Prestiges, jewelry.
2 - 3. Packaging for San Giorgio Olive Oil.
4 - 5. Food Packaging for smoked salmon.
6. Wine label for Villa Ragazzi.
7. Packaging for Flowers of the World candy.

100

1. Poster for "Concept" design symposium.
2. Invitation for restaurant opening.
3 - 7. Stationery, menu and matches, take-out packaging, wine labels for Ristorante Palio D'Asti.

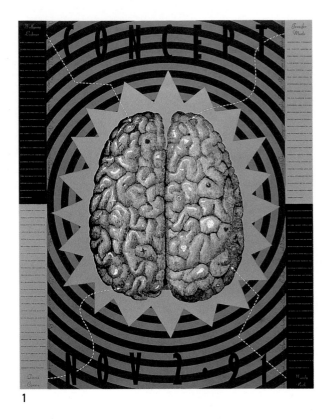

1

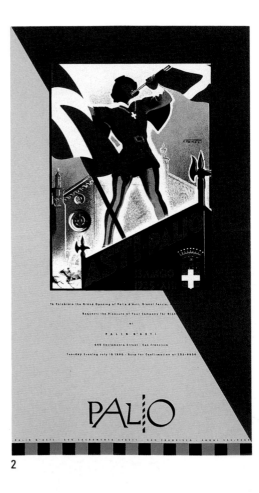

2

3

4

5

6

7

CRAIG FRAZIER DESIGN

"Design isn't about what something looks like, it's about what people think when they see it," says Craig Frazier. A strong believer in the early tenets of advertising legend David Ogilvy, Frazier seeks to evoke a response whether designing an ad, brochure, trademark, or poster.

Craig Frazier's work can be as whimsical as The Alphabet Critter Playbook or as serious as a corporate ad campaign. Clients like Steelcase, Trimble Navigation and LucasArts look to Frazier Design to create materials that differentiate them.

"Our struggle is to do hard working design for every client," says Frazier. Whether the design uses words, drawings photographs, or type, Craig Frazier is after "a clear message that achieves tangible business results."

1

2

The 1988 World's Most Memorable Poster
Jan 24-Feb 8 Western Merchandise Mart

The "1988 World's Most Memorable
Poster" will be displayed in the Center for
Design of the West, in Merchandise
Mart. The exhibition, which will preview
on Tuesday, January 24th, with an open-
ing cocktail reception at 5:30 p.m., is a
collection of winning entries in the Third
Third Annual International Poster Design
Competition representing the work of
800 artists from 60 countries.

Nine posters represent the work of
American Designers. Five were produced
by Bay Area Designers Michael Vanderbyl,
Craig Frazier, Tim Bruce and Michael
Schwab, and Stephen Suitor and Jose Ortega.
Other American winners include Seymour
Chwast, Steff Geissbuhler, James McMullan
and Tim Russell.

The poster competitions are organized
in association with UNESCO, the United
Nations Educational, Scientific and
Cultural Organization, and are judged on
the basis of combining quality of graphic
design, impact, authenticity and global
appreciation.

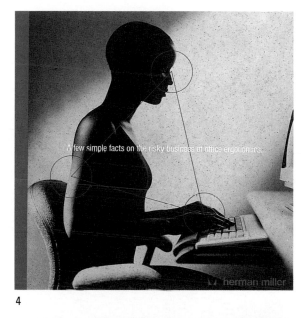

4

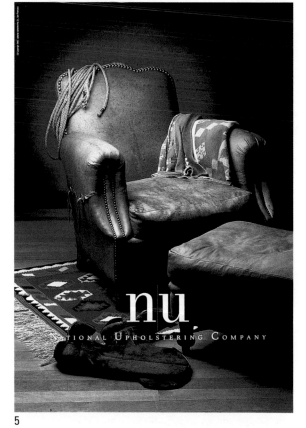

5

1. Frazier Design.
2. Brochure for Renaissance Software.
3. Poster for Unesco Poster Show.
4. Book on office ergonomics.
5. Ad for National Upholstering Company.

103

1

2

3

5

X is for xenopod,
exactly like a frog.

T is for tiger,
with terrific teeth.

B is for bear,
big and brave.

O is for otter,
on top of the ocean.

1 - 3. Poster series for Display
Lettering and Copy.
4. Logo for Agnes Bourne Furniture.
5. V is for Vulture, detail from
<u>Alphabet</u> <u>Critters</u>.
6. Spreads from <u>Alphabet</u> <u>Critters</u>,
a children's book.

K is for koala,
kind enough to kiss.

6

AGNES BOURNE

4

106

Function: Convert the esoteric to the practical.

1

2

3

4

6

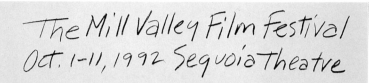

The Mill Valley Film Festival
Oct. 1-11, 1992 Sequoia Theatre

7

1 - 2. Corporate newsletter for
Trimble Navigation.
3. Illustration from book of
personal work.
4. Brochure for an accounting firm.
5. Poster for The Mill Valley
Film Festival.
6. Logo for Art Projects,
a contemporary art museum
in Sydney, Australia.
7. Ad for Steelcase furniture.
8. Logo for LucasArts Entertainment.

5

8

108

1

OPEN SYSTEMS SERVICES

Amdahl bridges the worlds of separate computing systems.

3

2

Privado. *Professional hair care products made from all the trusted secrets of style, health and beauty.*

Enriching Shampoo
FOR DAILY CARE
OF VIRGIN HAIR

Conditioning Shampoo
FOR PERMED/COLOR TREATED HAIR

Revitalizing Shampoo
FOR DEEP CLEANSING
ALL HAIR TYPES

Therapeutic Treatment
FOR DRY/DAMAGED
AND TREATED HAIR

Instant Conditioner
FOR DAILY CARE
OF ALL HAIR TYPES

4

1. Logo for Interstar Releasing,
a film company.
2. Illustration book of personal work.
3. Service portfolio for Amdahl.
4. Hair care products packaging.

INGALLS + ASSOCIATES

Figuring out what will make you pick up a book and get from beginning to end has been Tom Ingalls stock in trade since he put together the 450 page "David O. Selznick's Hollywood" for Alfred Knopf. The project took five years from start to finish and gave Ingalls an apprenticeship in book design that has served him well since.

Ingalls calls his efforts "graphic design with a view. "Books have a front door, an entry way, a living room and so on," says Ingalls. Deciding the mood of each room is his task. "You shouldn't notice the design, it should just illuminate the contents," he says.

Describing book design as a form of product packaging, Ingalls packages everything from cookbooks to book ideas and in-house magazines. Beyond the printed page the studio also designs packaging for everything from caviar to computer technology.

110

PHOTO: DEBORAH JONES

1

2

3

4

1. Tom Ingalls.
2. Ingalls + Associates
presentation folder.
3. Brandy labeling.
4. Wine labels.
5. Restaurant identity.
6. Caviar packaging.

5

6

1

1. Book covers.
2. Book design.
3. Cookbook design.
4. Book catalogs.
5. Magazine cover.
6. Book covers.
7. Arboretum Society
membership brochure.

2

3

5

4

6

7

114

1. Levi Strauss & Co. employee magazine.
2. Magazine cover.
3. Magazine cover.
4. Magazine cover.
5. Magazine cover, CD package.
6. Book cover.
7. Magazine covers.
8. Book cover.

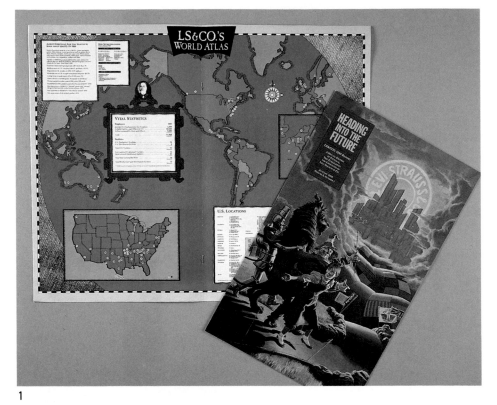

1

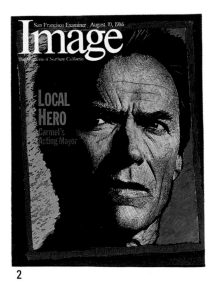

2

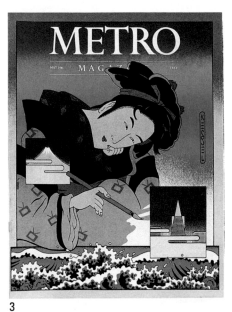

3

4

5

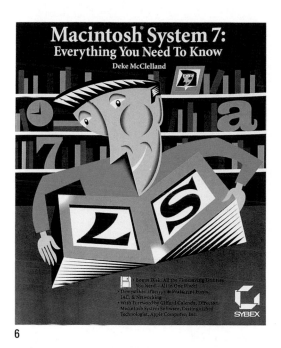

6

7

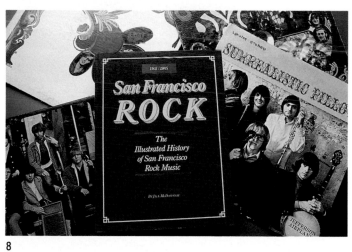

8

116

1

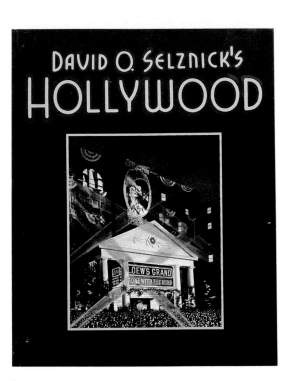

2

3

1. Book design.
2. Book design.
3. Book design.

118

It's hard to go anywhere in the world and not encounter a Landor design. The airline you fly, the hotel you stay at, the food you eat, the car you drive, all may bear Landor developed identities. Coca Cola, British Airways, Shell Oil, the '96 Olympics - the list and variety of work done at Landor Associates is endless.

Though enormous in scope and capability, Landor Associates maintains a family-like culture dating back to the days when Landor Associates was the Russian Hill cottage of Walter Landor and his wife Josephine. Growing from there to a ferry boat on the San Francisco Bay, and now its block length building on Front Street, Landor has spawned so many design careers it is casually referred to as the Landor University of Design.

Today, Landor Associates is a worldwide design operation with offices in the United States, Europe, the Far East, Central and South America and the Middle East. It's success is a testimony to Walter Landor's philosophy, "Just put your heart and mind to what you want to do, and dare to dream . . ."

1

2

3

SATURN

5

4

6

7

1. Symbol for the 1996 Centennial
Olympic Games in Atlanta, Georgia.
2. Store Identity for Coca-Cola 5th Avenue.
3. Packaging for Bausch & Lomb
eye care products.
4. Gift tin for Teachers Scotch.
5. Corporate identity for GM's Saturn.
6. Identity for Hyatt Hotels Worldwide.
7. Packaging for Blue Diamond Growers.

120

1. Packaging for HEB Coffee.
2. Identity/name for Touchstone Films.
3. Packaging for Del Monte Salad Bar.
4. Identity for an entertainment corporation.
5. Packaging for HEB Dairy.
6. Brand identity for McDonalds Corporation and The Coca-Cola Company.
7. Identity for Japan Airlines.
8. Brand identity for Artage, Japanese men's health and beauty aids.
9. Mark for Ferruzzi, European agri-business company.
10. Identity for the World Wildlife Fund.

1

2

3

4

5

6

7

8

9

WWF

10

1

122

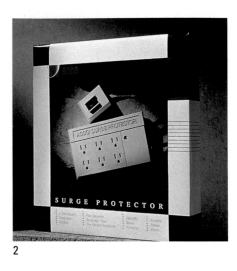

2

3

1. Corporate identity for Alcatel, French
telecommunications company.
2. Brand identity and package design
for Acco office products.
3. Packaging for Montevina Winery.
4. Identity program for CAT, industrial/
construction business.
5. Identity program for British Airways.
6. Identity for the Spanish Bank, La Caixa.
7. Packaging for Virginia Slims-Superslims.
8. Packaging for Lowreys Big Beef
beef jerky products.

4

5

7

8

6

L A N D O R   A S S O C I A T E S

1001 Front Street, San Francisco 94111   415.955.1400   FAX 415.956.5436

124

1

3

2

1. Packaging for Aviva Sport sports toys.
2. Packaging for Sutter Home Winery.
3. Mark for Levi's jeans and clothing.

LINDA LAWLER DESIGN

"One thing I like about design," says Linda Lawler, "is that it's a way of being anonymous and famous at the same time." With clients as recognizable as Levis and the San Francisco Museum of Modern Art, it's easy to understand what she means.

Though many clients at Lawler Design are in the high-visibility corporate league, Lawler says she often finds working with smaller non-corporate businesses most satisfying. "I'm very process-oriented, and the smaller-sized client generally allows me to become more involved with the project — to operate on a more personal level," she explains.

Over the past few years Linda Lawler finds herself increasingly drawn to clients in the fashion industry and the arts, providing them with a spectrum of design solutions ranging from promotional materials to packaging. Her approach is one of "redefining the wheel with each project," says Lawler. "Each problem calls for its own definition. The best part is when trying to find the solution becomes a treasure hunt."

1

2

3

1. Linda Lawler.
2. Olivia on the phone.
3. "Waste Not" poster for an AIGA, San Francisco, invitational exhibit about environmental issues.

128

1

2

3

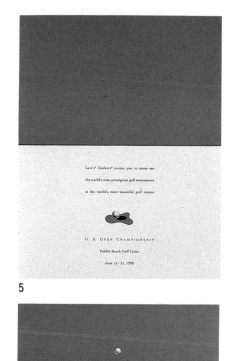

5

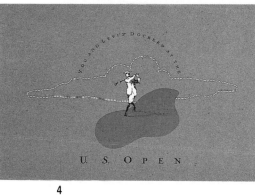

4

6

7

1. Catalog for Levi Strauss & Co.
2. Proposed hangtags for boys' wear.
3 - 6. Golf tournament invitation.
7. Hang tag.

2

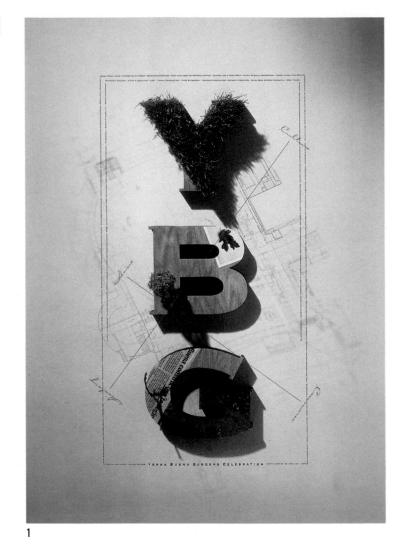

1

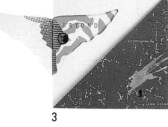

3

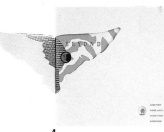

4

5

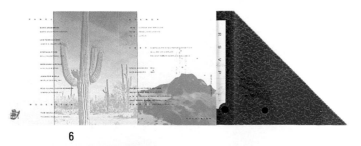

6

7

8

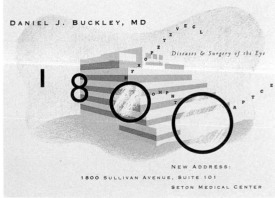

9

1. Poster for a lecture series on architecture and public art.
2 - 7. Invitation to a seminar on printing techniques.
8. Poster for a museum lecture series.
9. Moving announcement for an ophthalmologist.
10. Brochure inviting musicians to participate in a benefit tribute to John Lennon.

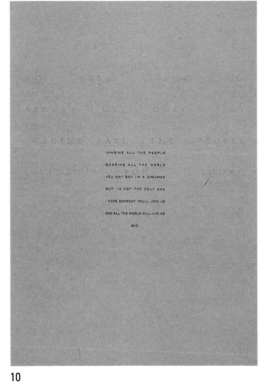

10

132

1

1. Invitation to a museum reception.
2. Commemorative bandanna and invitation for an art exhibition.
3. Catalog for a painting exhibition.

3

2

LISA LEVIN DESIGN

Coming from Los Angeles, Lisa Levin says she finds San Francisco "an inspirational place. I'm constantly in awe of the beautiful environment that I live and work in."

Lisa Levin Design consults on a broad range of design projects including annual reports, corporate identity, brochures, catalogues, signage and packaging for such diverse clients as Specialized Bicycles, The Nature Company, Shearson Lehman Hutton and The Bay Area Bioscience Center.

By keeping her creative staff small, Levin keeps a hand in every aspect of a project. "Design is a problem solving process for us. The more we learn about a client, the better work we do." Levin's goal is to achieve a balance between clarity that communicates and an artfulness that attracts attention.

1

2

3

4

5

6

1. Lisa Levin.
2. Promotional booklet for a photographer.
3. Hardbound datebook Christmas/
New Year's gift for a printer.
4 - 5. Cover and spreads for a tour book
for the Grateful Dead.
6. Logo and packaging for a men's
clothing store.

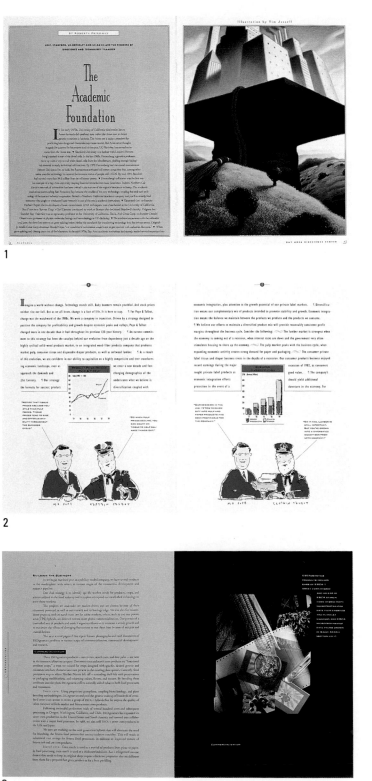

1. Spread from a corporate magazine about Northern California biosciences.
2. Spread from an annual report for Pope and Talbot, a forest products company.
3. Annual report spread for ESCAgenetics, a biotechnology company.
4. Clothing graphics for SEGA, a video game company.
5. Bicycle helmet packaging. Stacked boxes function as an instore display.

4

5

1. Product catalog for
S-Works high end bicycles.
2 - 4. Cover and spreads of
a double gatefold ad insert
for The Specialized Tire and
Rubber Company.
5 - 10. Covers and spreads
from various product and
accessories catalogs for
Specialized Bicycles.

1

2

3

4

5

6

7

8

9

10

140

1

1. Environmental poster for an AIGA/SF event.
2. Poster for the San Fracisco chapter of the AIGA's retrospective of the work of Jayme Odgers.

THE OFFICE OF MICHAEL MANWARING

"We call ourselves graphic designers, but only a third of what we do is printed graphics," says Michael Manwaring. The other two thirds involves applications of graphics to architecture.

"It's all communication," says Manwaring. "Whether it's a logo or the front of a building, it has to communicate everything that's inside."

San Francisco's Crocker Galleria is just one example of Manwaring's work in progress. And visitors to the famous wharfside Embarcadero will soon be enjoying the historical and interpretive signage he is busy designing for the San Francisco Arts Commission.

Projects that engage directly with the public pose Manwaring's favorite challenge; understanding public tastes while satisfying city officials.

142

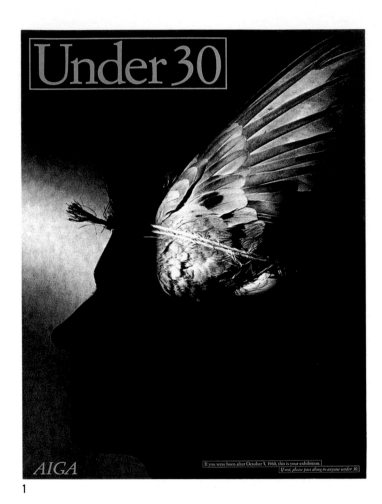

1

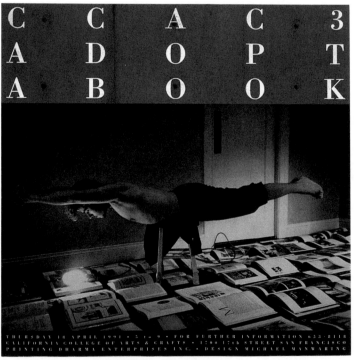

2

New American Furniture

3

4

5

1. AIGA poster/call for entries for an
exhibit of work by graphic designers
under 30 years old.
2. Poster for California College of
Arts & Crafts.
3. Logo for an exhibit at the
Oakland Museum.
4. Poster for a lecture presented by
AIGA, San Francisco.
5. AIGA poster for a local event on
environmental concerns.

144

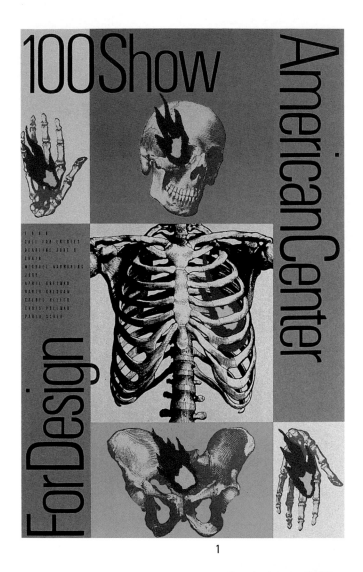

1

2

3

4

1. Call for entries poster for
American Center for Design 100 Show.
2 - 3. Logos for California College of Arts
& Crafts fund raising auction and barbeque.
4. Logo for San Francisco Print Council.
5. Design conference poster for Art
Directors & Artists Club of Sacramento.

ANNIBALE CARRACCI

146

2

1

1 - 2. Identification signing for a
San Jose museum.
3 - 4. Opera San Jose
identification signing.

3

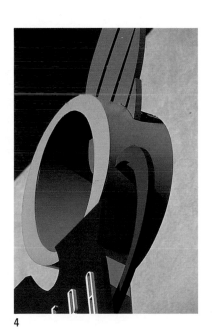

4

148

1

2

3

4

1- 4. Signing, entrance directories
and details at Rincon Center a
mixed use development.

MAUK DESIGN

Mitchell Mauk's fascination with three dimensional dynamics lives in the scrub brush wall that adorns his conference room as well as the studio's lighting fixtures. Both are Mauk inventions.

Mitchell Mauk credits youthful days with model trains and building blocks for a love of product design and graphic technology.

He's used three-dimensional graphics to create everything from MacWeek's interactive wall calendar to PG&E's trade show exhibit, which earned Mauk an Exhibit Designer of the Year award.

Aside from adapting technology Mauk enjoys making it understandable and identifiable across the full spectrum of communications vehicles, everything from print to signage.to interior design

"I try to do what's interesting." says Mauk.

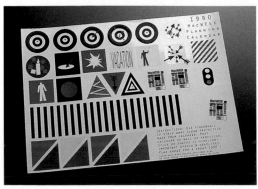

1

2

3

4

5

1. Mauk Design.
2 - 3. Media planning calendar and sheet of static cling stickers.
4 - 6. Brochure for a manufacturer of high fidelity speakers using typography as a visual metaphor for sound.

6

1

152

2

3

4

1. Logo for a company that sells and
services corporate jets.
2. Collateral system for Duncan Aviation.
3. Signing on company hangar.
4 - 5. Trade show exhibit for
Duncan Aviation.

5

1

2

1 - 2. Trade show exhibit for
software manufacturer.
3 - 4. Logo and signing for a retail
furniture dealer.
5. Literature bag for a magazine.
6. Signing for a typographer
slices through display window.

3

4

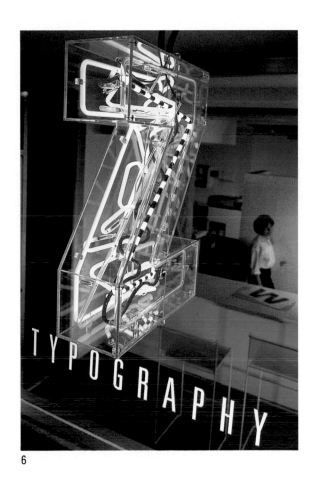

6

5

CURRY
GRAPHICS

1

2

3

4

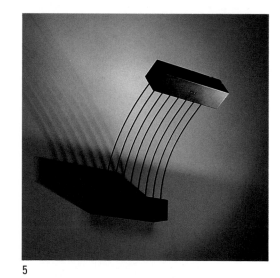

5

1. Logo for a silk screen printer.
2. Sales kit packaging.
3. Software packaging.
4. Invitation system for MacUser magazine.
5. Wall sconce light fixture produced in Italy by Artemide.

CLEMENT MOK DESIGNS

For high tech marketers who might think designers only know type Clement Mok designs is the answer. After 5-1/2 years at Apple Computer Clement Mok understands terms like "client-server object-oriented multimedia databases" the way most designers understand a layout.

In the scant five years since he left Apple, Clement Mok designs has become a 17-person firm enjoying the penthouse Bay view at San Francisco's Contract Design Center and designing everything from packaging to multimedia event graphics.

Years of turning hacker language into visual messages makes Mok as comfortable using technology as he is creating it's "look." "We have to be a filter as well as a translator for our client," he says. "Our niche is explaining the future and making the invisible visible."

158

1

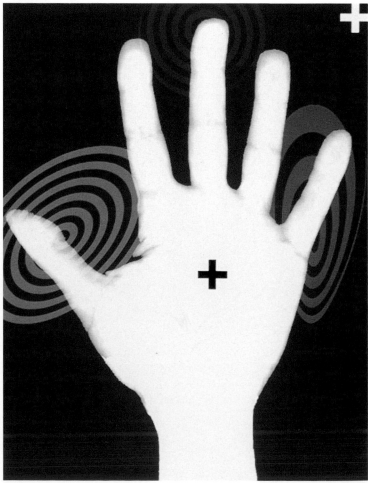

2

3

GAIN

4

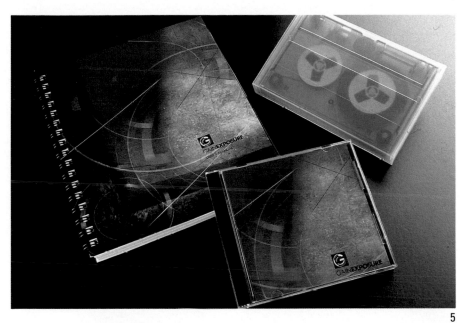

5

1. Clement Mok designs staff.
2. Studio logo.
3. Swirl hand illustration for New York Technical Summit.
4. Logo For GAIN.
5. Packaging for GAIN.
6. Logo on T-Shirts for Mirage Hotel.
7. Logo for Mirage Hotel.
8. Casino chips.

7

6

8

1

3

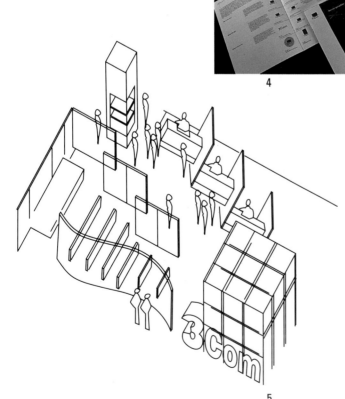

2

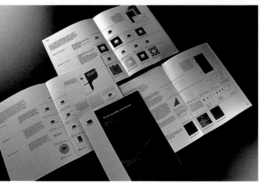

4

6

7

8

5

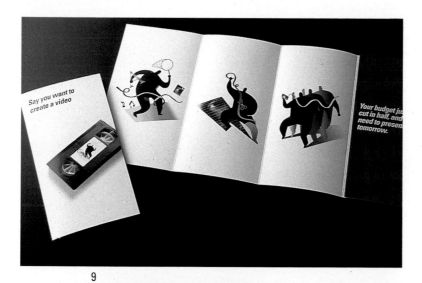

9

1. Logo for 3Com.
2. 3Com wrap logo.
3. Annual report, packaging and corporate materials for 3Com.
4. Basic Graphic Standards for 3Com.
5 - 8. Trade Show Booth for 3Com.
9. Brochure for Digital F/X Video.
10 - 11. Packaging and collateral material for Revo.

10

11

162

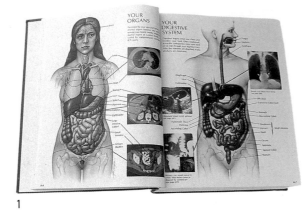

1

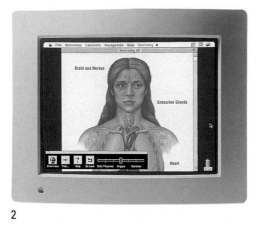

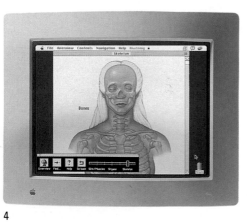

2

3

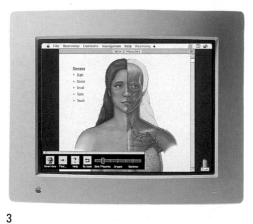

4

5

1 - 5. Mayo Clinic Interactive Family Health Book.
6. "Bug Eye Stare" Quicktime for Apple Computer.
7. "MacAerobic" Quicktime for Apple Computer.
8. MacAerobics Monologue transcript.
9. Quicktime CD-ROM for Apple Computer.
10. "Something Completely Different" Quicktime
for Apple Computer.

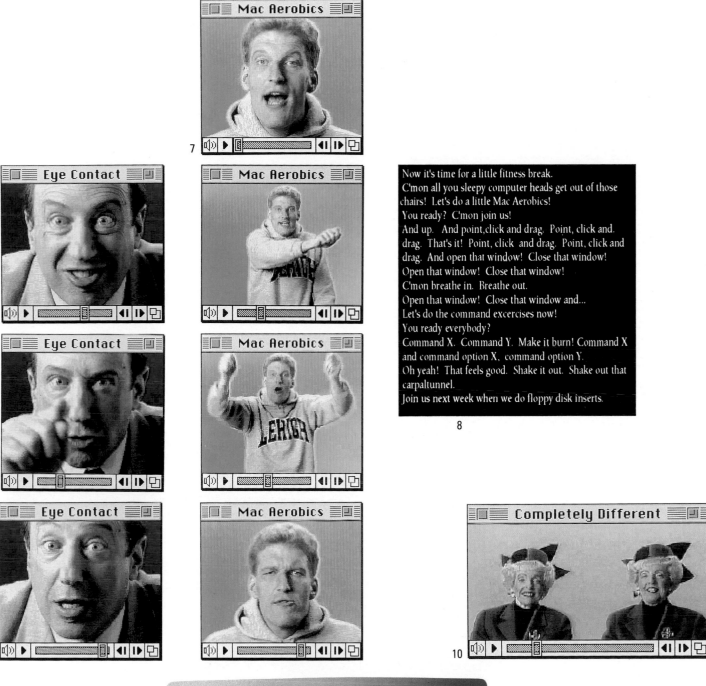

163

Mac Aerobics

7

Eye Contact

Mac Aerobics

6

Now it's time for a little fitness break.
C'mon all you sleepy computer heads get out of those
chairs! Let's do a little Mac Aerobics!
You ready? C'mon join us!
And up.   And point, click and drag. Point, click and.
drag. That's it! Point, click and drag. Point, click and
drag. And open that window! Close that window!
Open that window! Close that window!
C'mon breathe in. Breathe out.
Open that window! Close that window and...
Let's do the command excercises now!
You ready everybody?
Command X. Command Y. Make it burn! Command X
and command option X, command option Y.
Oh yeah! That feels good. Shake it out. Shake out that
carpaltunnel.
Join us next week when we do floppy disk inserts.

8

Eye Contact

Mac Aerobics

LEHIGH

Eye Contact

Mac Aerobics

Completely Different

10

9

600 Townsend Street, Penthouse, San Francisco 94103   415.703.9900   FAX 415.703.9901

1

164

2

1. WWDC 92 logo for
Apple Developer Group.
2. Banners for Apple
conference.
3. Packaging for
Macromind Software.

3

MORLA DESIGN

In 1984 Jennifer Morla formed Morla Design as a multifaceted design firm. Their creative services encompass print collateral, packaging, identity and logo development, video art direction and interior architectural design. Morla sees a fundamental aspect of her design approach as the creation of a total identity that suits a variety of mediums.

Jennifer Morla's images for Levi Strauss range from posters to fixturing, furnishings and department store interiors. Other projects at Morla Design include animated sequences for MTV, record album packaging, Swatch Watch designs, and numerous identity campaigns for experimental art organizations and museums.

166

1

2

3

4

5

1. Morla Design.
2. Jennifer Morla and staff.
3. Poster for Museum of Modern Art
series on radical design.
4 - 5. Announcements for an
experimental art gallery.

168

1

2

3

4

1. CD packaging.
2. Poster for Stanford
Conference on Design.
3. Menu and matchbook
for a restaurant.
4. Packaging for Cocolat
gourmet chocolates.
5 - 7. Levi's Kids Jean Shop
and fixture design.
8 - 9. Posters for Levi
Strauss & Co.
10. Brochure for
Levi's jeans.

5

8

9

6

7

10

Wells Fargo Bank

1

2

3

4

5

6

7

8

9

10

1. Logo for Wells Fargo Bank.
2. Credit cards for Wells Fargo Bank.
3. Brochure system.
4. Opening graphics for MTV Sports.
5. Logo for a casual Italian restaurant.
6. Logo for a children's sandcastle building event.
7. Poster to create a historic appreciation for Futura typeface.
8. Poster for Museum of Modern Art.
9. Annual report for San Francisco International Airport.
10. A condensed history of the art of writing for Simpson Paper.

172

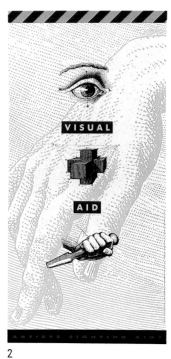

1. Catalog for Capp Street Project,
an experimental art venue.
2. AIDS awareness poster.
3. Environmental education poster
for American Institute of Graphic Arts.

YASHI OKITA DESIGN

Yashi Okita calls himself a marketing oriented graphic designer. "I don't design just for my satisfaction as a designer. If the product doesn't sell, then it's not a good design," he explains.

Okita's career began as an ad agency art director hiring graphic designers to develop his concepts. "But I enjoyed the hands-on work of mechanicals and drawing, even to the point of doing work myself that was supposed to go to the production department," he says. It wasn't long before he was starting his own design firm.

The firm began with a mix of 75% advertising projects and 25% design. Today the reverse is true. Okita and his five-person staff design corporate literature and collateral for financial, high-tech and medical institutions. With the usual array of computer equipment close at hand Okita says "I still enjoy the feel of cut and paste."

174

1

2

3

4

5

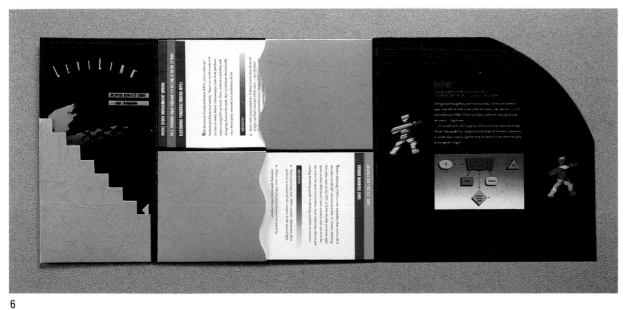

6

1. Yashi Okita Design staff.
2. Studio logo.
3 - 4. Materials for Levi Strauss & Co.
Human Resource Department.
5 - 6. Logo, brochure and presentation
folder for LeviLinkWorldwide Service.

176

1

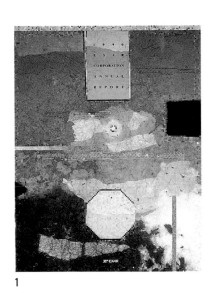

2

3

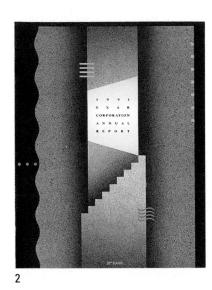

4

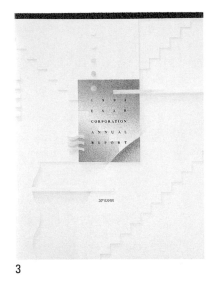

5

1 - 3. Annual report cover designs
for Exar Corporation.
4 - 5. Brochures for Exar Corporation.
6. Logo and poster for video game
tournament for Sega of America.
7 - 10. Capability brochure for Taxan
Corporation.

6

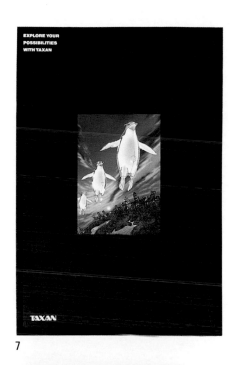

7

8

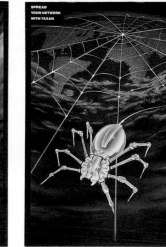

9

10

1

2

3

4

5

6

1. Capability brochure for
Stanford Hospital.
2. Loudspeaker brochure for
Blakeslee Design.
3. Capability brochure for
Hitachi Data System.
4. Package design for Tiny Brown
Corporation V-JET modem.
5 - 6. Corporate brochure/catalog
for Echelon Corporation.
7. Brochures for Hewlett Packard
customer support programs.
8. Package design for Micro
Processor Evaluation Kits.

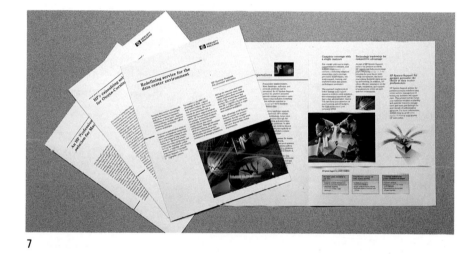

7

8

180

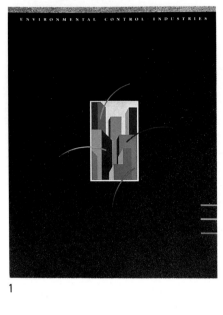

1

2

4

3

1 - 3. Capability brochure.
4. Brochure for Intel Corporation.
5. Product logo for Intel Corporation.
6. Logo for Bezier Corporation.
7. Logo for Direct Marketing Group.

5.

 BÉZIER   6.

 DIRECT   7.

MICHAEL OSBORNE DESIGN

"We love to design," is Michael Osborne's simple description of the approach at Michael Osborne Design. "We like to meet our client's objectives, to arrive at a solution based entirely on the problem,".

At Michael Osborne Design they meet design objectives for everyone from Shasta Beverages to Bank of America, Hewlett Packard, and San Francisco's gourmet favorite Trader Vic's. When they're not serving high-end corporate clients Osborne makes an intentional effort to meet the needs of pro-bono clients like the Children's Home Society, the San Francisco Ballet and Marin's Italian Film Festival.

"Our goal is to solve design problems without imposing a design style for a diverse mix of clients," says Osborne. "If we succeed in solving the problem, and win an award, well that's the best of all worlds."

182

1

MICHAEL **OSBORNE** DESIGN

2

3

WINTOOLS™

THE WINDOWS™ CUSTOMIZATION SYSTEM™

Turn Windows into a true OBJECT-ORIENTED environm

Decrease training and support needs by making co

use of the GRAPHICAL ENVIRONMENT. Expand dra

to its full potential. Create easy-to-understan

CUSTOMIZED ICONS. Automate functions with keystroke

macros. Organize functions on up to 16 virtual screens.

WinTools. POWERFUL. Easy to use.

1. Michael Osborne.
2. Studio logotype.
3. Label design for promotional Christmas gift.
4. Packaging for Windows Software

1

2

3

5

6

7

8

4

9

1. Collateral materials for the
San Francisco Show entitled
"A Salute to Creative Inspiration".
2. Promotional poster.
3. Packaging for a microbrewery.
4. Proprietary wine label for a
video game manufacturer.
5 - 8. Greeting cards for One Heart Press,
Osborne's letterpress shop.
9. Logo design.

186

1

1. Packaging design for a soft drink line.
2. Packaging for beef jerky.
3. Poster for a printer, reflecting personality test results.
4. Software package and display/shipper for a screen saver program.
5. Logo for a color separator.
6. Logo for an entertainment company.
7. Logo for a printer.
8. Logo design.

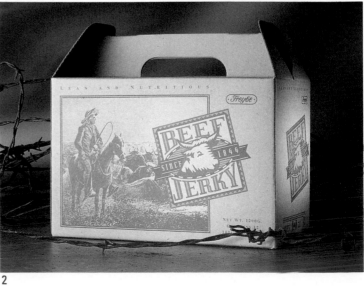

2

3

P I X X O N

5

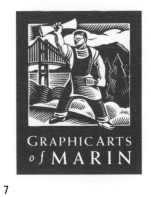

imagineer

6

4

GRAPHIC ARTS
of MARIN

7

AMERICAN CRAFT COUNCIL

8

M I C H A E L O S B O R N E D E S I G N

539 Bryant Street, San Francisco 94107   415.495.4292   FAX 415.495.0285

188

1. Packaging for an isotonic sports drink.
2. Packaging design for a line of
bartending products.
3. Poster for a printer.

1

3

2

PENTAGRAM DESIGN

190

1

With locations in San Francisco, New York, and London, Pentagram harnesses a formidable international resource of design teams within one organization. "There is the potential for a collaboration of talent from all of the offices," says San Francisco's Neil Shakery.

Partners at Pentagram manage their own staffs and projects and are responsible for bringing in their own business. At Pentagram San Francisco partners Kit Hinrichs, Neil Shakery and Lowell Williams head up three design teams handling everything from corporate identity and collateral to editorial design, packaging and environmental design and signing.

Learning and sharing are important aspects of working here," says Shakery. Pentagram's design teams are "hardly isolated from one another," he continues.

It is not an exaggeration Shakery says to call Pentagram "a unique organization." At Pentagram there is no boss, no hierarchy, no senior partner, no business partners — just designers.

2

Pentagram

3

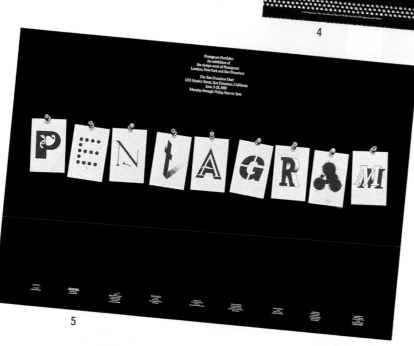

4

5

8

6

7

1. Pentagram partners (l.to r.) Kit Hinrichs, Neil Shakery and Lowell Williams.
2. Bi annual review of the work of the Pentagram Partners in London, New York and San Francisco.
3. Pentagram logo.
4. Compilation of designers' and illustrators' interpretations of the American flag.
5. Poster for an exhibit of studio work.
6. Merger announcement for an engineering firm.
7. Portfolio for an antique statuary dealer.
8. Symbol for the Royal Viking Queen cruise ship.

196

1. Poster for a benefit run.
2. Tabloid magazine for Art Center
College of Design.
3. Symbol for the San Diego Museum
of Contemporary Art.

THE 1987 HALLOWEEN
FIRST REPUBLICBANK SYMPHONY CLASSIC

1

2

3

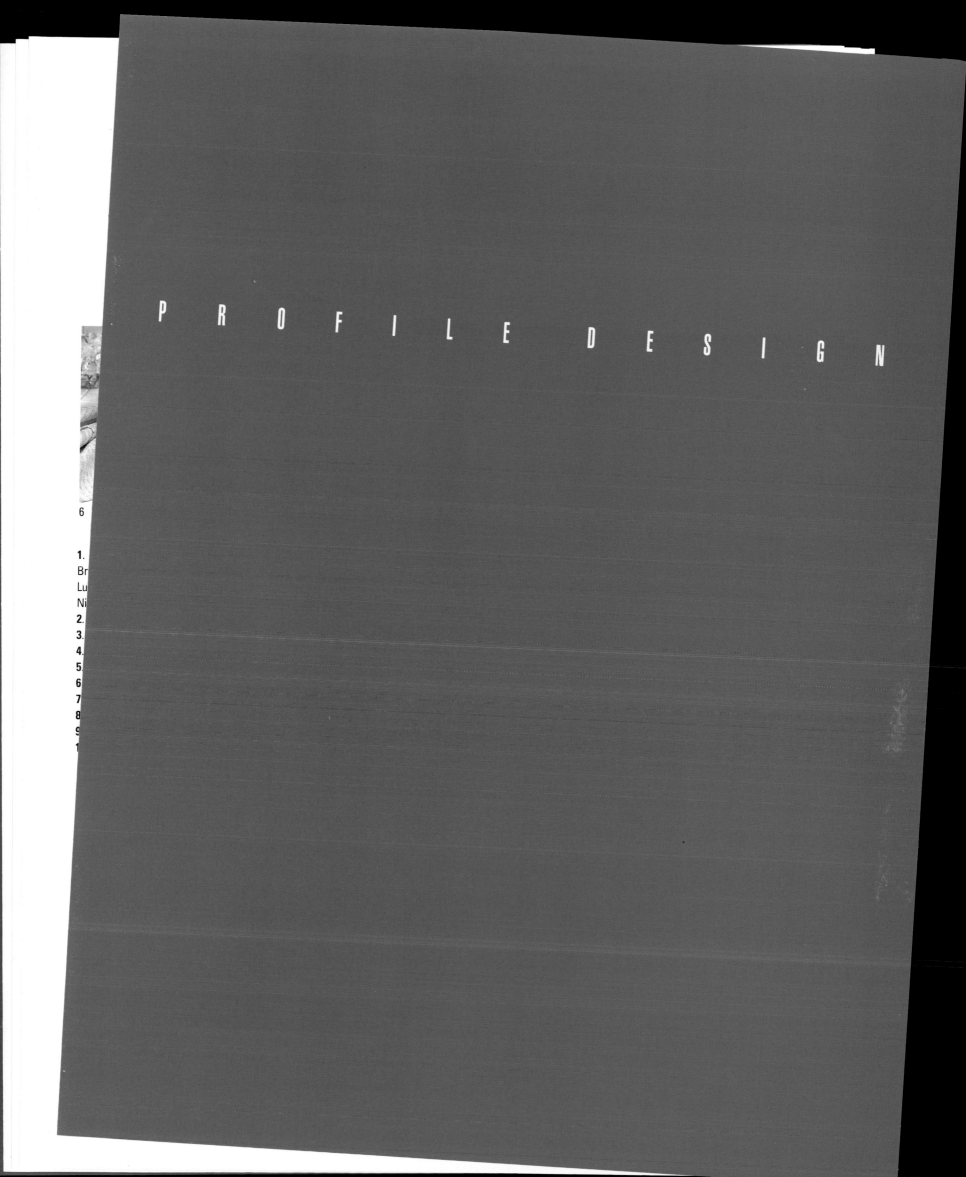

PROFILE DESIGN

6

1.
Br
Lu
Ni
2.
3.
4.
5.
6
7
8
9
1

P R

198

206

Gerald Reis & Company enjoys a central
downtown Sutter Street location nearby San
Francisco's fashionable Union Square shopping neighborhood.

Adept at everything from environmental design
to print graphics, product design, and packaging
Gerald Reis & Company has served the wide
ranging needs of developers, restauranteurs,
automobile and furniture manufacturers and the
clothing industry.

Reis credits right hand assistant Albert Treskin
for much of their success in symbols and trade-
marks. "We have a shared passion for typography," he says.

"People come to us for a unique approach," says
Reis. "We can work with The Nature Company
and General Motors at the same time because
with each situation we'll arrive at a new, fresh,
untested approach."

1

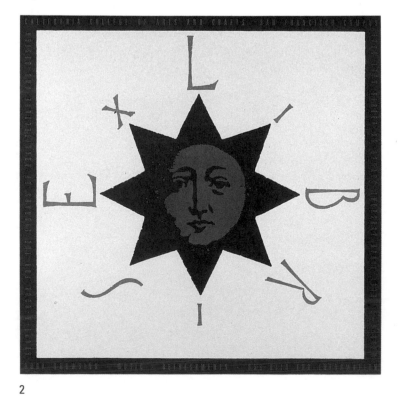

2

1. Gerald Reis and staff.
2. Poster for an Adopt-A-Book program at California College of Arts & Crafts.
3. Poster for the San Francisco Print & Design Council.

210

1

2

3

1. Gift boxes for The Nature Company.
2. Mask of recycled images for
Simpson Paper.
3. Symbol for Figura.
4. Show house poster for DIFFA/Design
Industries Foundation for AIDS.

211

4

After leaving Kansas City for San Francisco in 1988, Mark Sackett took just eight months to move from doing freelance projects for Landor and Chiat Day to opening a studio of his own.

A commitment to take each client's objectives to heart is reflected in the versatility of Sackett's portfolio. "We don't have battles with clients over creative control. They know we take their best interests to heart," Sackett explains.

Sackett Design's work encompasses corporate identity, product styling, packaging design, apparel, editorial design, and all forms of collateral. The unifying element, he says, is "hard work and appropriate solutions."

Sackett's 2,000 square foot studio is memorable for its forty six collections of antique toys, game boards, dolls, and packaging. Brightly colored circus posters line the walls, along with shelves of everything from cigar boxes to children's toys. Such typographical and packaging memorabilia provide not only design inspiration but Sackett says lend a playful balance for all that "hard work."

214

1

2

3

4

1. Mark Sackett.
2. Studio logo.
3. Posters for the California Crafts Museum.
4. Packaging for meat products.
5 - 6. Hang tags and labels for Levi Strauss & Company.
7. Poster for a ballet production.

7

5

6

216

1

2

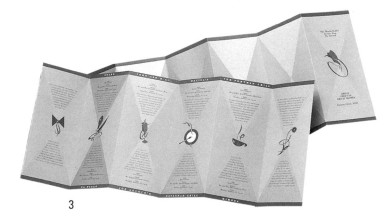

3

4

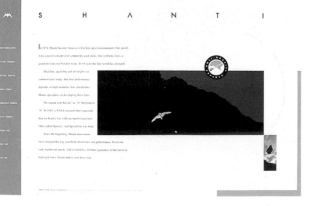

4

5

6

7

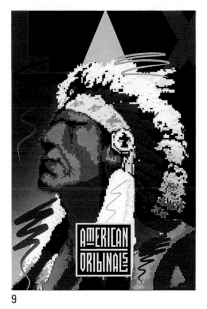

9

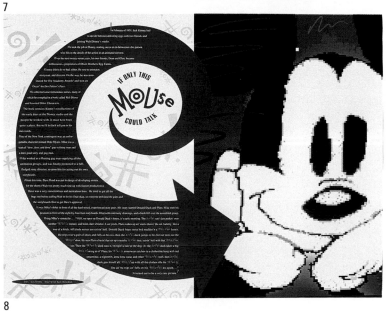

8

1. Product labeling for Levi Strauss
& Company jeans.
2. Poster for a printer to benefit
the Animal Legal Defense Fund.
3. Direct mail/invitation for
The Marin Ballet.
4. Logo and advertising for
Shanti Kite Products.
5. Point of sale materials for
Levi Strauss & Company.
6 - 9. Editorial design for LAX
Magazine-- Language, Art,
Expression.

1

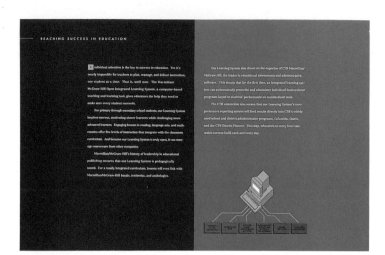

2

3

4

5

6

7

9

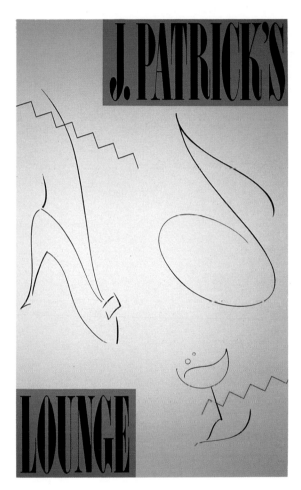

8

10

12

1 - 3. Corporate brochure for an educational software product.
4. Logo for Young Imaginations.
5 - 7. Capabilities brochure for Soma Chiropractic.
8. Lounge poster for Hyatt Hotels.
9. Logo for The Starr Group.
10. Product labeling for a new product.
11. Poster for the annual bay area creative show.
12. Awards certificates for The San Francisco Show.
13. Logo for Nova Financial Services.

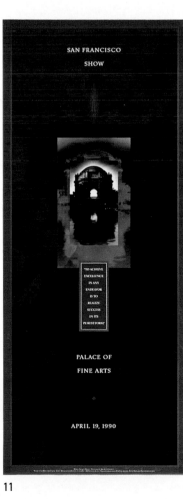

11

13

220

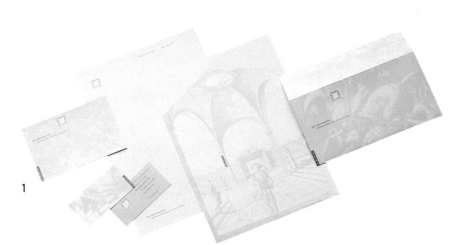

1. Stationery system for an art gallery.
2. Logo for Child Care Employee Project.
3. Logo for Suppers, a restaurant.
4. Logo for an art gallery.
5. Logo for Wheeler Audio Associates.
6. Logo for duty free shops.
7. Logo for The Porter Group , a family benefits organization.
8 - 9. Direct mail/invitation for the Marin Ballet.

2

3

4

5

6

7

8

9

MICHAEL SCHWAB DESIGN

222

After twelve years in San Francisco Michael Schwab finds rowing on the Bay outside his Sausalito waterfront studio and riding a bike to work preferable to fighting for a downtown parking spot. "Here, I can drive or ride right up to my door," he says.

Healthy images, portrayed as straightforward, simple statements have become Schwab's hallmark. An illustrator and graphic designer, Schwab's images serve the needs of everyone from Apple Computer, Coca Cola and Levi Strauss to Sports Illustrated, Esprit, Eddie Bauer and the San Francisco Opera.

Clients go to Schwab for his signature style. A style that uses bold colors and equally bold images to make what he calls "a simple, clean, powerful statement as quickly and succinctly as possible."

1

2

PHOTO: ROGER LEE

3

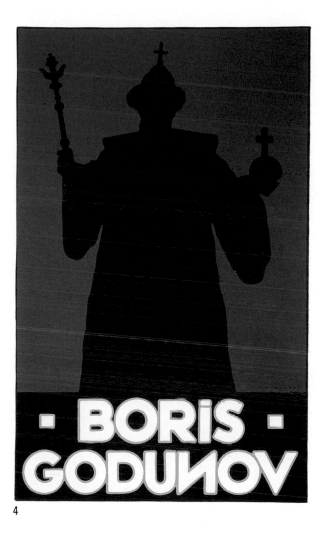

4

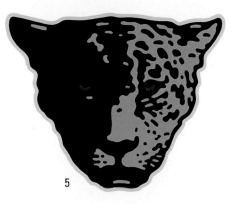

5

1. Michael Schwab.
2. Promotional material.
3. Poster for AIGA Environmental Project.
4. Poster for San Francisco Opera.
5 Calendar image for Paragraphics
Fine Printing.

224

1

2

3

1. Poster for Texas Aqua Festival
2. "Mannequin" - American
Showcase book cover.
3. Recruitment poster for Oklahoma
State University rowing team.
4 - 7. Trade show graphics
for Sun Microsystems, Inc.

4

5

6

7

226

1

2

1. Poster for HMS Queen Elizabeth II.
2. Poster for Denver Polo Cup.
3. Logo for a film production company
4. Book cover and poster for
Walt Disney Publications.

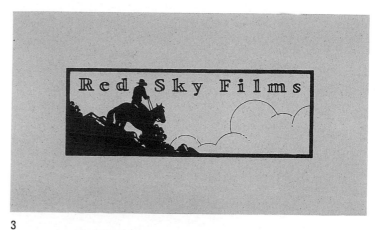

3

4

228

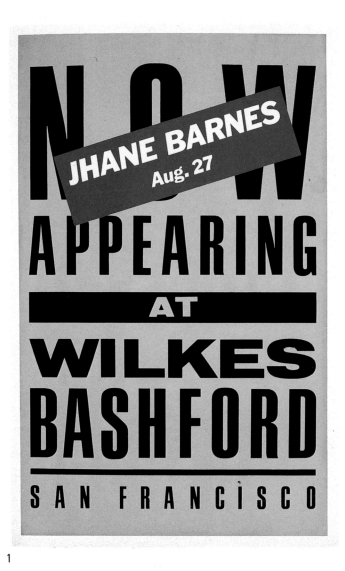

2

1

A BOY

ERIC MICHAEL

SCHWAB

Born to Kathryn & Michael

FEBRUARY 27

1   9   8   5

3

1. Poster for a men's clothier.
2. Logo for Robert Bruce Woolens,
a sweater manufacturer.
3. Birth announcement.

SAM SMIDT

1

Clients drop into Sam Smidt's studio like they were visiting "Cheers." Smidt gives a wave from his helm at the back of the studio.

At "Cheers" they may act like family, but at Sam Smidt's studio some of them <u>are</u> family. Daughter and designer Becca Smidt recently came on board, and for years Smidt's wife Marlene has done everything from write copy to balance the books.

For the six designers on staff, the studio's open layout lends itself to a collaborative approach. "As a studio we try to change all the time yet maintain a maturity and sophistication," to create appropriate design solutions that are contemporary without being trendy," says Smidt. "If a client is willing to pay for design, they ought to get an original idea," he concludes.

Those original ideas have served everyone from universities to retail chains, computer companies and art organizations. Eye-catching ads, fashion hang tags, fabrics, furniture, books, packaging and posters, all have won Smidt awards. As one client put it "Sam is creative with a twist. He'll have an idea that'll hit you as surprising, shocking, different - more than just a good idea.

2

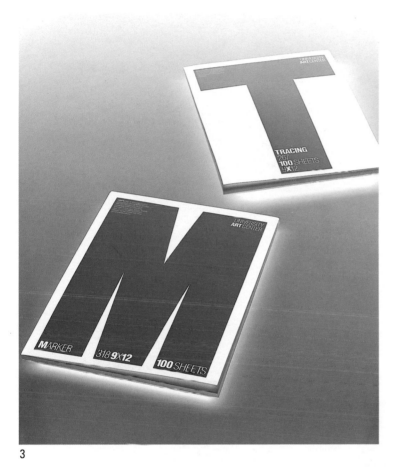

3

1. Sam Smidt.
2. Shopping bag for an art supply store.
3 - 4. All purpose art pads.
5 - 6. Ads for a ladies boutique.

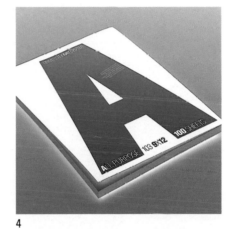

4

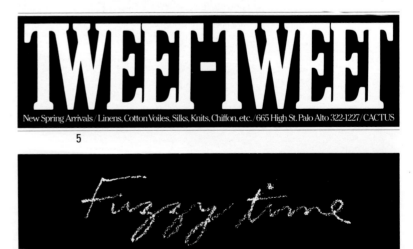

5

6

1

2

4

3

5

6

7

1. Presentation kit for a
clothing company.
2 - 4. Outdoor signage for an
apartment complex.
5. Graphics for a laundry room.
6. Integrated presentation system for
a computer company.
7. Vehicle signage.
8. Hang tags for a clothing
manufacturer.

8

234

2

1

4

3

5

1. Brochure for a Japanese
clothing company.
2 - 5. The Santa Monica Series, a line of
 interior design fabrics and wallcoverings.
6. Manuals and desk stand for
a computer company.
7. Gift box product design.
8. Sculpture catalog for the San Francisco
Museum of Modern Art.
9. Packaging for a retail chain.
10. Shopping bag for a retail chain.

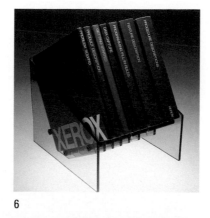

6

7

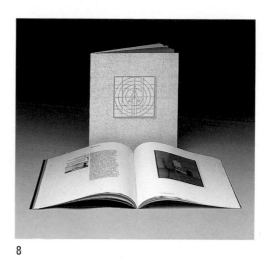

8

9

10

236

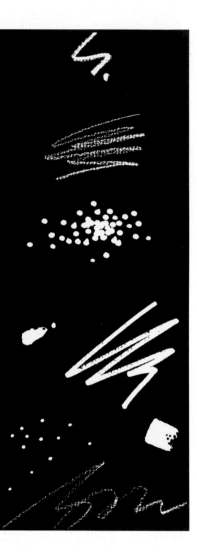

1

1. Ad for a high end audio-video retailer.
2. Logo for Alexian Brothers Catholic Hospital.
3. Logo for a design group.
4. Logo for a clothing line.
5. Logo for a ladies boutique.
6. Logo for Palo Alto Cultural Center.
7. Logo for a construction company.

2

3

4

5

6

7

TENAZAS DESIGN

Lucille Tenazas' reputation in design made it to San Francisco while she was still in New York. Now principal of Tenazas Design, her design work spans 16 years, two continents and two coasts.

Tenazas Design creates identity systems and communications design projects for institutions, corporations, arts organizations and business, among them James River Corporation, Royal Viking Line and the University Art Museum, University of California Berkeley.

Intentionally keeping her studio small, with a staff of just three including herself, Tenazas enjoys taking personal responsibility for every aspect of a project. "I have to have my hand in everything," she says.

"I've always been fascinated by communication and the strength of language," she says. "I listen carefully to clients, but at the same time I listen to my own voice."

238

1

2

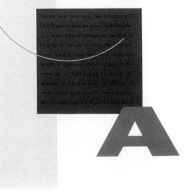

3

4

1. Identity system for Center for the Arts at Yerba Buena Cardens.
2.- 3. Cover and spread for the Center for the Arts.
4. Membership brochure for the. Pacific Film Archive.
5. Calendar of events for Pacific Film Archive.

University Art Museum

March   April 1991   University of California at Berkeley
                          2625 Durant Avenue, Berkeley, CA. 94720

A Bimonthly Calendar

Pacific Film Archive

The Banned and the Beautiful

Czech and Slovak Filmmaking 1963 – 1972

MATRIX

Kiki Smith

Zoe Leonard

Lewis deSoto

Pacific Film Archive

Japan: New Generation

Early Ozu

The Bat: *A Comedy-Mystery-Drama*
April 1, Castro Theater, Dennis James at the Organ

The **Independent Group:**

Postwar Britain and the Aesthetics of Plenty

5

240

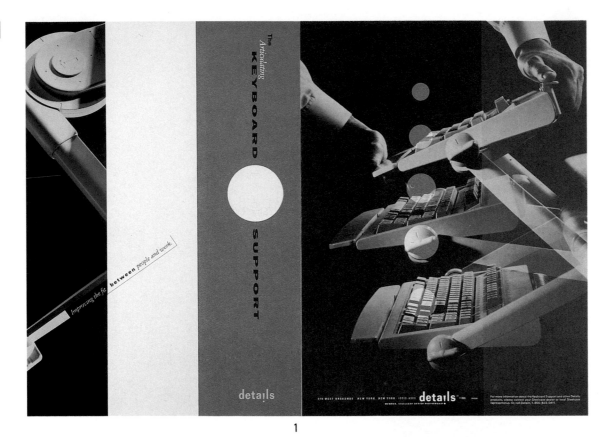

1

2

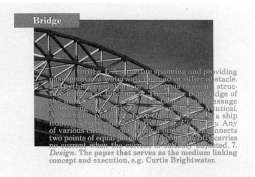

Bridge [brij] *n.* 1. A structure spanning and providing passage over a waterway, railroad or other obstacle. 2. Anything resembling or analogous to such a structure in form or function. 3. *Anat.* The bony ridge of the human nose. 4. *Music.* A thin, upright piece of wood in some stringed instruments over which the strings are stretched. 5. *Naut.* A crosswise platform above the main deck of a ship from which the ship is controlled. 6. *Electricity.* Any of various circuits containing a branch that connects two points of equal potential and consequently carries no current when the circuit is suitably adjusted. 7. *Design.* The paper that serves as the medium linking concept and execution, e.g. Curtis Brightwater.

3

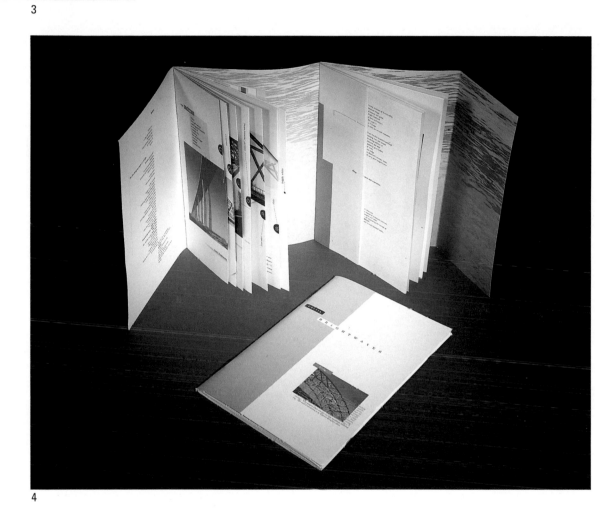

4

1 - 2. Product brochure for the Articulating
Keyboard Support, a Steelcase product.
3. Detail of a brochure, depicting bridges
as its theme, for a paper manufacturer.
4. Brochure illustrating the capabilities of a
printing paper.

1

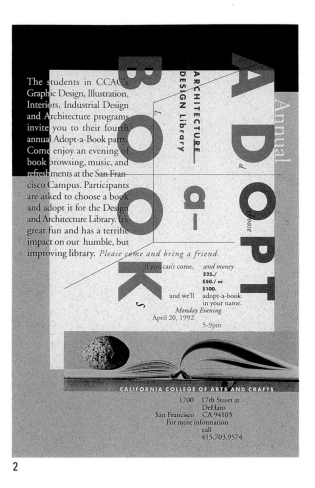

2

1. Poster for Center for Critical Architecture
Art and Architecture Exhibition Space.
2. Announcement postcard.
3. Call for entries poster for Art and Architecture
Exhibition Space.

244

1 - 4. Promotional brochure for a paper company entitled Visions.

1

3

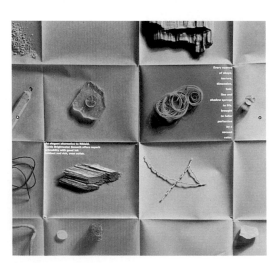

2

4

THARP DID IT

THARP DID IT gets its noteworthy name from designer Rick Tharp. Established in 1975, THARP DID IT is as likely to "do it" for a restaurant next door as a corporation across the globe. Serving clients from Sweden, Australia and California's Napa and Silicon Valleys, the five-person studio has won everything from a free meal to a CLIO.

Rick Tharp's penchant for breaking the rules includes making the ordinarily lifeless UPC bar code yet another form of graphic identity. For Sebastiani Vineyard's "Eye of the Swan" wine label, Tharp casually transformed the UPC into marsh reeds befitting its label theme. According to Tharp, "We don't break rules just to be breaking rules, but on the other hand, we don't let them get in the way either."

Most of THARP DID IT's work is in the disciplines of corporate and retail visual identity and environmental and package design. While the studio's client base has grown internationally, its philosophy remains refreshingly provincial. It's a philosophy that says "always have fun doing it."

246

2

1

PHOTO:F.L.AVERY

Ⓣ

3

0 88232 42032 2

4

1. Rick Tharp.
2. The design studio.
3. Labeling for Sebastiani Vineyards.
4. UPC bar code as illustration.
5. Print ad for a winery.
6 - 7. Architectural graphics and symbol for Bakeries by the Bay.
8. Logo for retail fruit stores.
9. Symbol for Bon Appetit, a catering and event production company.
10. Logo for retail housewares stores.
11. Icon for Cinnamon Schnapps "Fire & Ice" packaging.

5

6

7

CASA de FRUTA

SINCE 1908

8

9

DOMUS

10

11

248

1

2

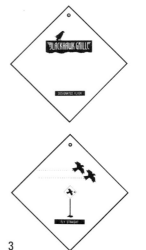

3

1. Architectural detailing of a restaurant.
2. Restaurant logotype.
3. Cocktail napkins urging prudent consumption.
4. Bolo tie worn by waiters.
5. Wine label.
6. Detail of entry.
7. Wine list for Cafe Del Rey.
8. Wine label.
9. Signing for a restaurant.
10. Interior detail.

4

6

5

7

9

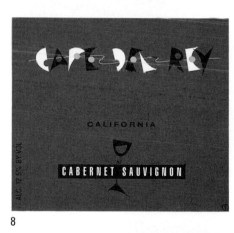

8

10

The letterforms of the logo
are based on the shape of
the barrel-backed chairs in
the dining room.

1

250

1. Logotype for a chain of bakeries.
2. Packaging for Le Boulanger.
3. Exterior signage.
4. Restroom identification.
5. Interior detail.
6. Magazine cover.
7. Symbol for a novelty candy product .
8. Proposed shoe packaging made of recycled materials.
9. Wine label and original art.
10. Packaging for Hewlett-Packard desktop printers.
11. Wine label.

2

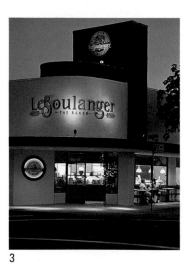

4

3

5

6

7

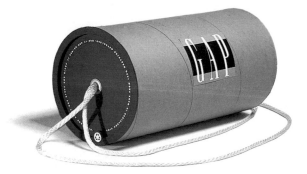

8

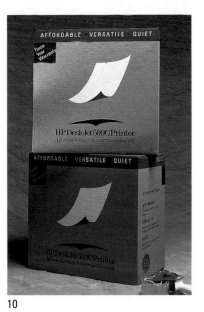

9

10

11

252

2

1

Imagination is more important than knowledge. BRIO

Give them roots and give them wings BRIO

To play is to learn BRIO

Discovery is what growing up is all about. BRIO

3

4

1. Ad and illustration for a wine organization.
2 - 3. Catalog and posters for a Swedish
toy company.
4. Icon for a paper seminar, "Michael,
Jennifer & Kit On Paper".

VANDERBYL DESIGN

From furniture, to linens, retail stores to product showrooms, since its inception in 1973 Vanderbyl Design has made a habit of stretching the boundaries of graphic design and continues to seek out new areas to explore.

A strong believer in long term client relationships, most client tenures with Vanderbyl Design span four to ten years.

254

Among those clients who've benefited from such lengthy relationships are Esprit, Bernhardt Furniture Company, IBM, Polaroid, Hickory Business Furniture, Robert Talbott Company and the Kronos Quartet.

"Design doesn't stop at the two dimensional page," says Michael Vanderbyl. Interlocking design disciplines, Vanderbyl looks to provide clients with a total identity, expressed in "all aspects of what a company does." Whether it's a showroom, fabric, furniture, catalogue, ad or retail interior, the goal at Vanderbyl Design is "to harness all materials to say one thing."

1

2

3

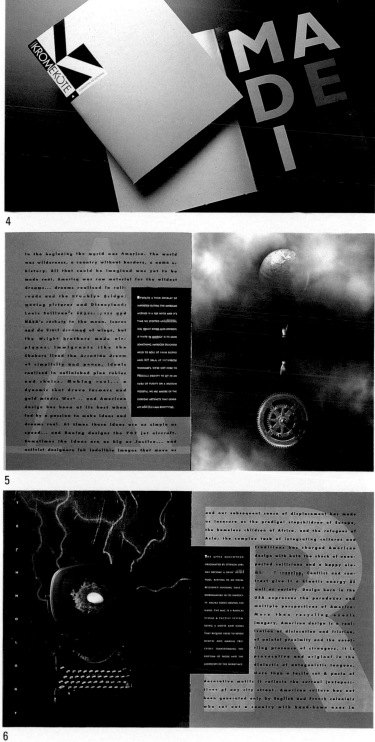

4

5

6

1. Brochure for textile line based on patterns found in the New York subway.
2. Bernhardt Furniture Company's Chicago showroom.
3. Logo for a residential development overlooking a flower growing region.
4 - 6. Paper promotion brochure entitled Made in America.

256

1. Hickory Business Furniture Chicago's showroom.
2. Poster for California College of Arts & Crafts opening of gallery space.
3. Brochure system and product binder for a furniture manufacturer.
4 - 5. Annual report.
6 - 7. Annual report.
8. Logo for Lascaux, a restaurant.

1

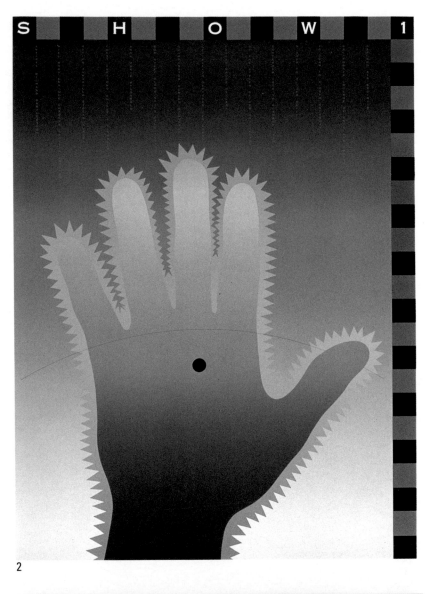
2

3

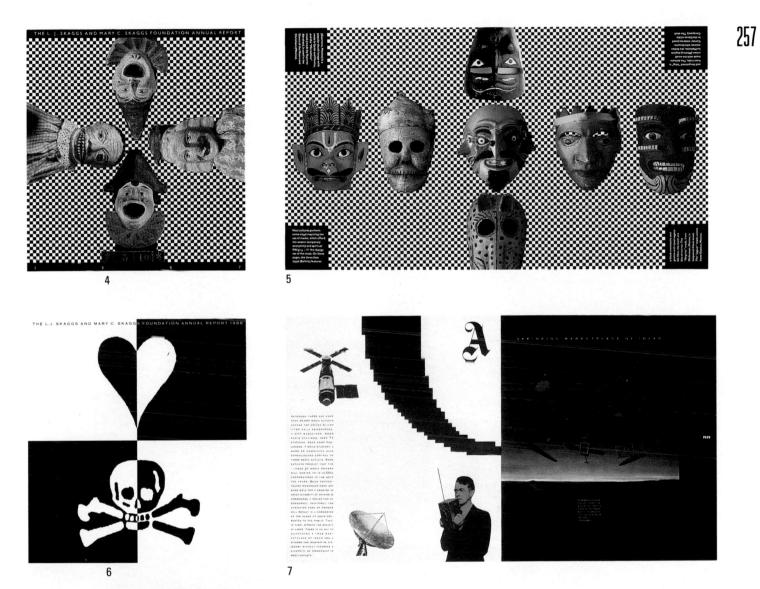

4

5

6

7

8

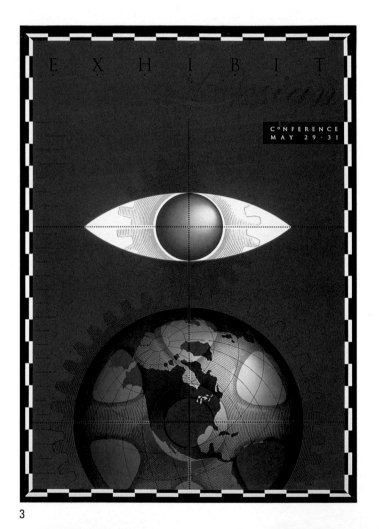

1

2

3

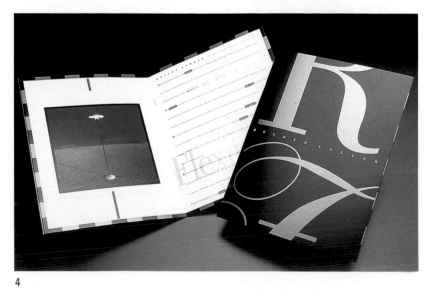

4

5

1. Poster for Polaroid.
2. Logo for a residential development in Hawaii, Makani Kai, which means ocean breeze.
3. Poster/mailer for Design Conference exhibit.
4. Corporate identity brochure.
5. Delivery truck for a typographer.
6. Stationery system designed to show various typefaces used.
7. Furniture line brochure.
8. Logo for a silk screening company.

6

7

8

260

1

2

1 - 2. Kids' bed sheet design
and brochure.
3 - 4. New York shoe showroom.
5. Bedsheets and packaging
design.

3

4

ZIMMERMANN CROWE DESIGN

How do two graduates of East Carolina University wind up directing street smart Levi's videos in San Francisco? For Dennis Crowe and Neal Zimmermann it was inevitable. "We were attracted to the level of professional respect many San Francisco graphic designers command in the business community," says Zimmermann.

Using video as an exciting tool, Crowe calls it "the language of our generation." "Neal and I both enjoy working with a variety of media," he says.

The firm often combines identities, posters, in-store displays, bus shelters, billboards, radio and TV ads into cohesive programs for their clients.

Zimmermann Crowe Design looks for clients who have the savvy to appreciate great design and the courage to use it; and they've found many in San Francisco.

262

1

2

3

1. Zesty Coffee Delight holiday gift for clients and friends of Zimmermann Crowe Design.
2. Symbol for Zimmermann Crowe Design.
3. Dennis Crowe, Neal Zimmermann and staff.
4. Direct mail fall image piece for International Youth Apparel.
5. Calendar gift-with-purchase for International Youth Apparel.
6. Growth chart gift-with-purchase.
7. Gift-with-purchase package includes pencils, post cards, stickers and a note pad.

4

5

6

7

1

2

3

1. In-store display unit for Levi's Capital E jeans.
2. Display unit (mannequin version) for Levi's Capital E jeans.
3. The back of both display units.
4. Levi's Capital E book.
5. Booklet hang tag for Levi's Shirts.
6. Trade image piece for Levi's Shirts.
7. Retail sell-in kit for Levi's Shirts.
8. Symbol for Club 4808, a heavy-metal night spot.
9. Symbol for Hero Presentation Printing.
10. Mark for International Youth Apparel winter clothing.

4

5

6

7

8

9

10

266

1

4

1 - 4. Cover and various spreads for
Levi's Sweats image piece.
5. Trademark for Levi's Sweats.
6. Sell-in video and :30 television spot
for Levi's Sweats.
7 - 9. Point-of-sale posters for Levi's Sweats.

2

3

5

6

7

8

9

INDEX

MAUK DESIGN
636 Fourth Street
San Francisco 94107
415.243.9277
FAX 415.243.9278

CLEMENT MOK DESIGNS, INC.
600 Townsend Street
Penthouse
San Francisco 94103
415.703.9900
FAX 415.703.9901

MORLA DESIGN, INC.
463 Bryant Street
San Francisco 94107
415.543.6548
FAX 415.543.7214

YASHI OKITA DESIGN
2325 Third Street
Suite220
San Francisco 94107
415.255.6100
FAX 415.255.6300

MICHAEL OSBORNE DESIGN
539 Bryant Street
San Francisco 94107
415.495.4292
FAX 415.495.0205

PENTAGRAM DESIGN
620 Davis Street
San Francisco 94111
415.981.6612
FAX 415.981.1826

PROFILE DESIGN
151 Townsend Street
San Francisco 94107
415.979.0780
FAX 415.979.0781

GERALD REIS & COMPANY
560 Sutter Street
San Francisco 94102
415.421.1232
FAX 415.421.5706

SACKETT DESIGN
864 Folsom Street
San Francisco 94107
415.543.1590
FAX 415.543.2860

MICHAEL SCHWAB DESIGN
80 Liberty Ship Way #7
Sausalito 94965
415.331.7621
FAX 415.331.7623

SAM SMIDT, INC.
666 High Street
Palo Alto 94301
415.327.0707
FAX 415.327.0699

TENAZAS DESIGN
605 Third Street
Suite 208
San Francisco 94107
415.957.1311
FAX 415.957.0707

THARP DID IT
50 University Avenue
Suite 21
Los Gatos 95030
408.354.6726
FAX 408.354.1450

VANDERBYL DESIGN
539 Bryant Street
4th floor
San Francisco 94107
415.543.8447
FAX 415.543.9058

ZIMMERMANN CROWE DESIGN
90 Tehama Street
San Francisco 94105
415.777.5560
FAX 415.777.0370

This book would not have
been possible without those who
contributed the impressive
selection of work represented here.

I would like to specially thank
Michael Vanderbyl for his essay
and R.J. Muna whose photographs
begin the book, as well as all those
who put their efforts into providing
me with the information needed to
produce San Francisco:Graphic Design

Among those who deserve
particular recognition for their
contribution are Anita Bennett,
Bruce Tillman and Lisa Woodard
for their design and production
assistance.